Policing
Las Vegas

Other Books by Dennis N. Griffin

The Morgue

Red Gold

Blood Money

Killer In Pair-A-Dice

One-Armed Bandit

Pension

Policing
Las Vegas

A History of Law Enforcement
in Southern Nevada

Dennis N. Griffin

Huntington Press
Las Vegas, Nevada

Policing Las Vegas
A History of Law Enforcement in Southern Nevada

Published by
Huntington Press
3687 S. Procyon Ave.
Las Vegas, NV 89103
Phone (702) 252-0655
e-mail: books@huntingtonpress.com

ISBN: 0-929712-23-4

Cover Design: Laurie Shaw
Interior Design & Production: Laurie Shaw

All photos, except those listed below, courtesy of the Las Vegas Metropolitan Police Department.

Additional photo credits: Metropolitan Police Museum of Nevada, Inc. pgs. xv, xvi (lower right), 1, 2, 5, 12 (bottom), 15, 20 (lower left), 21 (upper right), 33, 40, 46, 53, 54, 83 (right), 158, 159, 161; Kent Clifford pg. 57; Dwight Mahan pgs. 74, 169, 170, 171, 173; David Groover pg. 92; Mike Bunker pg. 96; Enrique Hernandez pg. 145; Dennis N. Griffin pgs. 153, 157, 163; Edward Jensen pg. 166; Georganne Lee pg. 176; Eric Cooper pg. 179; Nina Radetich pg. 183.

Dedication

To the men and women, sworn and civilian, of the Las Vegas Metropolitan Police Department and its predecessors, the Las Vegas Police Department and the Clark County Sheriff's Department. They have, through their professionalism and integrity, made Las Vegas and Clark County a safer place for us all.

Acknowledgments

This book would not have been possible without the help of many people who were willing to rummage through old files, share their documents and photos, and take the time to tell me their stories. To all of them, my heartfelt thanks.

The Las Vegas Metropolitan Police Department was particularly cooperative and supportive. I extend my special gratitude to former Undersheriff Richard Winget, who was instrumental in helping me locate information and steering me in the right direction when my research bogged down. Carol Swift, of the Office of the Sheriff, provided details that were critical in preparing the timeline of events, as well as photos.

The Metropolitan Police Museum Association of Nevada, Inc., was another vital resource. The information and photos they made available were invaluable to me.

The Clark County Library and its newspaper archives supplied important facts and insights. Many articles from the *Las Vegas Sun* and *Las Vegas Review-Journal* contributed to my understanding of various incidents and events. A 1983 series of articles by the *Los Angeles Times* was particularly enlightening when researching the history of Anthony Spilotro and his reign as a Las Vegas crime boss. The Las Vegas Strip Historical Site was an additional source of information on the entertainment industry.

I hope those individuals and organizations I have mentioned by name, and the numerous others whom I have not, will be pleased with the finished product.

Contents

Preface

I moved to Las Vegas from central New York in 1994 after retiring as an investigator with the New York State Department of Health. Having spent the previous 20 years in law enforcement, it wasn't long before I found that I missed the action and excitement of my previous life. In an effort to maintain some ties to law enforcement, I joined the Metropolitan Police Department's Volunteer Program shortly after its inception in 1996. In 1998 I attended the Citizen Police Academy. Also in 1996, I started writing my first suspense/thriller novel, *The Morgue*.

In January 2002, with four books then in print, my interests in Metro and writing merged. An acquaintance I had met at a writers conference emailed me that her book about the history of the Indiana State Police had been published. That news planted a seed in my mind: Had anyone written the history of Metro?

Internet research failed to disclose the existence of such a book. My next step was to check with Metro. I was eventually directed to call the office of Undersheriff Richard Winget. When we spoke on the phone, he informed me that the only written history of Metro of which he was aware was a yearbook published in 1998, marking Metro's 25th anniversary. And this book was available only to Metro personnel, not the general public.

Encouraged that no one had beat me to it, I explained what I wanted to do. I also told Winget that I didn't see how my project could be successful without Metro's cooperation. It was agreed that I would prepare a written proposal detailing the project and present my plan to the Undersheriff for consideration and possible referral to his boss, Sheriff Jerry Keller. A few days later we met; that same day I had my answer: Sheriff Keller had approved my proposal and Metro would support my efforts. That cooperation continued under Sheriff Bill Young.

Starting with the establishment of Las Vegas in 1905, I began to put together the history of law enforcement efforts in the Las Vegas Valley. Using documents available through Metro, the library, and the Metropolitan Police Museum Association, I learned that "night watchmen" had been the predecessors to organized police forces. They were followed by the formation of the Las Vegas Police Department and the Clark County Sheriff's Department to provide police coverage for the City of Las Vegas and the unincorporated areas of Clark County. Those two agencies subsequently consolidated to form the current Las Vegas Metropolitan Police Department.

My initial research, while interesting, was sometimes frustrating. Information was sketchy and in some cases gaps existed in the continuity of service of the many chiefs of police and sheriffs. Also, in those early years many incidents cried out for more detail or clarification. Unfortunately, no one from that era was still alive to talk with.

Things improved as I reached the 1940s. I found three members of the Las Vegas Police Department still living in Las Vegas. Although they were up in age and long out of police work, they each agreed to talk with me and share their memories of what it was like to be a cop in Las Vegas back then. I found all three to be very sharp mentally and their stories were fascinating. I spent many enjoyable hours with these wonderful men, individually and as a group. Their interviews prompted me to add the "Recollections" section to the book. It contains the personal accounts of these old-timers and others who served, or were otherwise involved, with Metro much more recently.

As the timeline of events moved toward the present, I was able to expand on the historical reporting of specific incidents through interviews with the actual participants. The Rodney King riots—in which a small group of officers engaged in hand-to-hand combat with a mob of gang-bangers and thugs trying to reach the downtown casinos—was mesmerizing. The 1979 incident in which three convicted felons took over the jail and ended with two inmates dead and a guard wounded also captivated me. And then there is the story of the rookie cop who was shot six times in December 2002 and refused to die. These are but three examples of the acts of heroism I discovered.

I knew that no book about

policing in Sin City would be complete without a section on organized crime. I initially decided to direct my efforts toward the 1970s and 1980s, when mobsters controlled many of the casinos. Skimming money from these establishments provided a hefty source of income for several crime families across the country. Although these activities have been widely covered in books and television documentaries, I thought if I could speak with some of the agents and law-enforcement officers who had been involved in the various investigations, perhaps previously unreported information could be developed.

I was successful in contacting several retirees from a number of agencies that had investigated the casino skimming operations in one capacity or another. But this book was about Metro, so I concentrated on the street-crime aspects of the mob. There were murders, burglaries, robberies, and loan-sharking operations being committed or run by the mobsters during that same time period. These activities came more directly under Metro's area of responsibility. I found that one man was considered to be the kingpin in organized-crime's street activities. That man was Anthony Spilotro.

Tony Spilotro came to Vegas in 1971 to oversee the Chicago mob's interests. With a reputation of being capable of extreme brutality, he joined his old pal Lefty Rosenthal, who was already running the casino operations for the mob at the Stardust Hotel and Casino. Characters based on these two men are played by Joe Pesci and Robert De Niro in the movie *Casino*.

For the next 15 years Spilotro ruled over the criminal element in Las Vegas. According to records and information provided by the police officers involved, the story of the war between law enforcement and the gangs contains all the elements of a Hollywood thriller.

There were killings, one of which was allegedly a hit by the police. A contract was put out on two Metro officers, prompting their boss to fly to Chicago with a gun in his briefcase to confront the mob leaders. Cops and ex-cops went to work for Spilotro, providing protection and information. The Spilotro episode hasn't been told from the police point of view until now.

Although this book focuses on the history of Las Vegas from the police perspective, the needs and direction of policing efforts were tied to events in the gambling, entertainment, and tourist industries. Without their success in bringing tourists and new residents to the Valley, Las Vegas as we know it today wouldn't exist and there would be no need for an organization like the LVMPD. Therefore, brief mentions of events from the gambling and tourist world are interspersed throughout the book.

So, if you're interested in history, police history, or Las Vegas, I think you'll find this book to be a worthwhile read. I sincerely hope you enjoy it.

Introduction

Las Vegas (Spanish for "The Meadows") was officially founded as a city on May 15, 1905. The San Pedro, Los Angeles and Salt Lake Railroad auctioned off 1,200 lots in two days surrounding a central area that would later be known as "Glitter Gulch." The 40 square-block downtown section of modern-day Las Vegas was a railroad town and the railroad remained its principal industry for the next 25 years.

In the early days, Las Vegas was one of a handful of small towns in vast Lincoln County. In 1909 it became the county seat for the newly established Clark County.

In 1910, an anti-gambling law became effective in Nevada. The law was so strict that it even forbid flipping a coin for the price of a drink. Within weeks, however, underground gambling began to flourish all over the state, including little Las Vegas.

On March 16, 1911, Las Vegas became an incorpo-

First Commercial Establishment in Las Vegas—1904

rated city. It encompassed approximately 20 square miles and had a population of about 800. At the same time, Clark County had 3,321 residents.

By 1930 Las Vegas had grown to a population of 5,165. Shortly thereafter, three things occurred that permanently altered the city of Las Vegas, Clark County, and Nevada.

First, on March 19, 1931, gambling was legalized in Nevada. The bill approved by the legislature was authored by a northern Nevada rancher named Phil Tobin, who had never visited Las Vegas and had no personal interest in gambling. One month later, six gambling licenses were issued for Las Vegas, the first one going to Stocker's Northern Club on Fremont Street.

Second, state divorce laws were liberalized. With easier residency requirements, "quickie" divorces could be attained in only six weeks. Short-term residents flocked to the state. In Las Vegas, many of them stayed at dude ranches, the forerunners of the sprawling Strip hotels of today.

And third, the beginning of the construction of Hoover Dam generated a population boom and boosted the Valley's economy, which was in the grip of the Great Depression.

And of course, all of these events impacted the need for, and the direction of, policing in the Las Vegas Valley.

In 1933, the first of the Las Vegas celebrity weddings occurred when Johnny Weissmuller, who played Tarzan in the movies, married Lupe Valez.

Las Vegas railroad depot—1922

1

Las Vegas Police Department 1905-1973

Early Chiefs of Police

After the establishment of Las Vegas in 1905, law enforcement rested with a group of men known as night watchmen. They were responsible for keeping order in a town comprised primarily of rough miners and railroaders. A particularly troublesome area, Block 16, was located on the east side of First Street between Ogden and Stewart avenues, the only place in the young town where liquor and prostitution were allowed. Block 16 was well-known for frequent fights and shootouts.

The first few night watchmen hired were put out of com-

mission after sustaining severe beatings, and one officer was killed. Newly appointed night watchman Joe Mullholland was shot to death in October 1905. Mullholland got into an altercation with a man named William McCarty that resulted in McCarty being arrested

Outskirts of Las Vegas—1905

Block 16—1906

and taken to jail. After locking McCarty up, Mullholland became concerned that the cell was too cold and damp for the inmate to spend the night in. He relented and turned the prisoner loose. McCarty later caught up with Mullholland in Arthur Frye's Saloon and shot him dead.

In 1906, Block 16 saloon owners organized and demanded that the toughest man they could find be hired to maintain order in Block 16. That man was Sam Gay.

Sam Gay

Sam Gay was born on March 1, 1860, on Prince Edward Island in eastern Canada. Gay grew up in Massachusetts, then went out West, spending some time running a

wheat farm in North Dakota before moving on to San Diego, where he served as a conductor on the San Diego Electric Railroad. That was followed by a stint as a miner in Nome, Alaska, then a return to San Diego.

Over the next few years, Gay tried several trades. He worked as a City Marshal in Coronado, California, and as a gold miner in Goldfield, Nevada. He also worked as a bouncer at Tex Rickard's Northern Club in Goldfield. Rickard went on to promote some of the greatest boxing matches of the era.

In the autumn of 1905, Sam Gay arrived in the newly established City of Las Vegas. His first job was as a bouncer at the Arizona Club, located in Block 16. Gay was a big man, six feet and 260 pounds. He was fearless and very efficient with his fists. Gay shunned carrying a gun while on duty, relying on his verbal and physical skills instead.

His abilities soon came to the attention of Jake Johnson, Lincoln County Sheriff. In January 1906, Johnson appointed Gay as Night Officer for Las Vegas. As rough and tough as Block 16 was, Sam Gay was equal to the task. It is reported that Gay's technique to break up the numerous fights that occurred was to push his way through the invariable crowd of onlookers to the combatants. Once he identified the troublemakers, he grabbed them by the scruff of the neck and bashed their heads together. This procedure was repeated as necessary until the fighters submitted. If the battlers were especially stubborn, Gay dragged them outside, tied them together at a hitching post, and doused them with a hose until their attitudes improved.

But as hard as he was, Sam Gay was never known to abuse his authority or mistreat prisoners. On the contrary, he was often criticized for being too lenient. At any rate, Sam Gay was the right man at the right time for Las Vegas.

That same year, the city's first official jail was built at the end of Fremont Street (current site of the Plaza Hotel).

Two law-enforcement-related events of note occurred in 1908:

Sam Gay was appointed a Lincoln County Deputy Sheriff and a new corrugated-iron jail was built on Stewart Avenue between First and Second streets. The inmate housing area was referred to as the Blue Room. Cockroach infested and compared to the Black Hole of Calcutta, it was considered more of a deterrent to crime than the law-enforcement officers.

After incorporating in 1911, Las Vegas appointed Sam Gay to be its first Chief of Police. Gay held this position until 1914 (Sam's amazing career will be picked up again in the history of the Clark County Sheriff's Department).

Frank Wait

In 1914, Frank Wait took over as chief. Wait was born in South Dakota in 1880 and moved to

Frank Wait

Las Vegas in 1906. He worked as a carpenter before switching to prospecting during the Gold Rush era. He served multiple terms as Chief of Police, as well as stints as City Marshal, Undersheriff of Clark County, and Captain of the Guards at the Nevada State Prison in Carson City.

According to a 1950 newspaper article, Wait patrolled the streets of Las Vegas on an old black mare named Nancy Hanks. He and the horse became a familiar sight and a symbol of law and order. In his later years, he recalled that he frequently picked up drunks and put them on the horse for the trip to jail. Wait claimed that this method of transport was easier than trying to get an intoxicated man into a car.

During Wait's initial term, a sign of things to come occurred. In May 1920, the first airplane flight to Las Vegas was made. The plane, occupied by Randall Henderson, a newspaper editor from Blythe, California, and one Jack Beckley, flew in from Needles, California.

Frank Wait died in 1950.

Robert Lake

In 1927, Wait was succeeded by Robert Lake. Lake was born in 1889 in Ontario, California. He was nicknamed "Spud" because of his affinity for eating raw potatoes. Spud and his family moved to Las Vegas when he was a young boy. After serving in World War I, Spud returned to Las Vegas in 1917 and became a deputy sheriff. He left there in 1920 to become part of the three-man Las Vegas Police Department. The pay was $5 per day. There were no uniforms; badges were their only means of identification. The three officers carried Colt .45s.

During his time with the department, Lake made it a habit to arrest one type of criminal the other cops neglected: drug addicts. "I didn't like hopheads," Lake is

Robert Lake

quoted as saying. "I was about the only one who ever picked up any hopheads. The rest of them didn't bother with them."

Spud Lake left the department in 1929. He passed away in 1980 at the age of 91.

Percy Nash

The Las Vegas Police Department got its fourth Chief of Police in 1929. This time an Englishman, Percy Nash, assumed the reins.

Nash was born in London in 1874. His parents brought him to America when he was three years old, settling in Oregon. After spending several years in the Northern Frontier during the Alaska Gold Rush, he moved to Nevada in 1907. He worked in the gold mines of Goldfield and silver mines of Tonopah before joining the Nevada State Police.

After Spud Lake resigned, Las Vegas officials determined that the best way to solve their police problems was to seek a qualified candidate from outside the area; their search led them to Percy Nash. He was recruited and brought to Las Vegas to take over the department on January 28, 1929.

Nash was the first chief to occupy the department's new office on Second Street, between Fremont and Ogden. Formerly the residence of Dr. Roy Martin, walls were torn down to accommodate Nash's office, a booking room, and business office. A large room directly to the rear was transformed into a courtroom.

Independence Day in early Las Vegas

It was during Nash's term that the LVPD's first motorcycle officer arrived on the scene. R. K. "Bob" Zeimer had the honor of assuming that position in February 1929.

Nash stayed on the job until he was asked to resign in 1931. He refused to step down, claiming that his record was good and there was no reason to give up his position. Still, he was relieved of his duties on July 1, 1931.

After his police career was ended, Nash served as an inspector for the State Pure Food and Drugs Department and the Bureau of Weights and Measures. He was also the City Milk Inspector. Percy Nash died in 1937 at the age of 63.

Clay Williams

For Chief Nash's replacement, the city fathers decided to promote from within. Clay Williams was born in Elizabeth, West Virginia, on July 15, 1890. Williams had extensive law-enforcement experience prior to joining the LVPD as a Special Officer in November 1930. He served as Deputy Commissioner of Prohibition and as a deputy sheriff in West Virginia. He was a detective for four years in Miami Beach and worked as an officer for the Union Pacific Railroad. On July 1, 1931, just as Hoover Dam construction got underway and the Las Vegas population went through a boom, he took the helm of the LVPD when he was appointed as Acting Chief.

At the same time, staffing was increased from seven to nine officers. However, only two of the original seven were retained. The other five were fired.

According to a newspaper article on July 18, 1931, Chief Williams declared that the reorganization of the department was complete and ready to handle any situation. Three patrol districts had been created, running from Main to Fifth Street and Stewart to Bonneville. Officers on foot covered these zones. An officer in a car patrolled the rest of the city. In addition, police telephones were installed in various sections, which were expected to improve efficiency. It sounded like Williams

Clay Williams

was moving the department in the right direction.

However, in August 1932, Mayor E. W. Cragin suspended Chief Williams. According to a newspaper story, the stated reasons for this drastic action were because: "Of the continual dissatisfaction of the people with the manner in which the affairs of this department have been conducted. Of the internal dissension within the department, which has existed for several months and has continually grown worse to the detriment of the community as a whole. Of the utter disregard of the head of this department for carrying out instructions for the betterment of the department. Of the fact that interested individuals not connected with the city administration have had access to the most confidential affairs of the department."

The suspension was lifted later that year and Williams was allowed to resign. He passed away in 1945.

Lewis Hord and Orren Boggs

Lewis L. Hord replaced Williams in early August. Hord was 48 at the time and assumed the duties of Acting Chief, LVPD, after having been with the department for less than a year. Although he lobbied for a permanent appointment,

Orren Boggs

Hord was replaced two months later. He left the department after that and was named the local Director of Public Relations for the Los Angeles Bureau of Power and Light Power Line, which was under construction in Clark County at the time.

On October 5, 1932, Orren Clinton Boggs was appointed as the next Chief of Police. Born in Ohio in 1876, Boggs was a pioneer businessman in early Las Vegas. He and his brother, B. F. Boggs, established the firm of Boggs Brothers Groceries and built the Boggs Building at 319 Fremont Street, which housed the J.C. Penney Company.

Chief Boggs was fired in 1935 after a change in city government. He passed away in 1947 at age 71.

The Police Department
Through The '40s

Musical Chairs

In January 1934, with legalized casino gambling in Las Vegas thriving and the population increasing to 7,000 from the influx of dam workers, the LVPD took a major step toward modernization. According to an article appearing in the *Las Vegas Age* on January 27, the department's two patrol cars were about to become radio equipped. "The receiving set has been placed in one car and tests performed have proved successful. The other car will be equipped soon," the story read.

For the rest of the '30s, two men alternated as Chief of Police.

Dave Mackey

One man held the office three times, his replacement occupied it twice.

On June 16, 1935, Dave Mackey became the new Chief of Police. Born in Gold Hill, Nevada, in 1896, he received his early education in Terre Haute, Indiana. He joined the police force there and served for several years before moving to Las Vegas in 1923. After five years as a car salesman, he went to work for the LVPD in 1928.

Mackey served multiple terms as chief. His first ended in 1937, when he resigned to return to his previous rank of Captain. Former Chief of Police Frank Wait replaced him; later that same year, Wait again left the department, albeit temporarily, and Mackey was reinstated. This time he served until August 1939. His replacement was none other than Frank Wait.

This third and final appearance of Frank Wait as head of the LVPD began on August 1, 1939. It ended in October 1941 when Wait was fired for allegedly failing to follow orders from the city fathers to clean up Block 16.

During Wait's last term, the population of Las Vegas reached 8,422. The LVPD increased its complement of officers from 12 to 14 in December 1939 by adding two "relief patrolmen." These extra personnel were hired in order to decrease the shifts being worked by existing officers from 12 hours to eight hours.

Also on Wait's watch, the first African-American police officer was hired by the Las Vegas Police Department. An officer named Cortez (first name unknown) joined the force in 1940.

Upon Wait's termination, Dave Mackey was yet again ap-

First LVPD Officer Killed

On June 8, 1933, Officer Ernest "Ernie" May became the first LVPD officer to make the ultimate sacrifice in the line of duty. At approximately 7:45 that evening, the station received a report of a disturbance at the Clark Auto Court on South Fifth Street. Officer May, just coming on duty, took the call.

Ernest May

When he arrived at the auto court, May discovered W. H. Clark, the 47-year-old owner and proprietor, intoxicated, armed with two handguns, and holding a woman hostage. A gunfight ensued during which both Officer May and W. H. Clark received mortal wounds, with both men dying at the scene. May's actions saved the life of the hostage and protected the safety of the other auto court residents.

City Constable Joe May, Ernest's brother, responded to the auto court a short time later and found both bodies.

There have been multiple versions as to exactly what happened that night and for decades the story was steeped in controversy. The evidence developed during the investigation and at the inquest showed conclusively that Officer May acted heroically and according to LVPD protocol.

Ernie May was 37 at the time of his death and had been an LVPD police officer for about three years. His widow and seven children, ranging in age from 15 years to six weeks, survived him.

pointed Chief of Police. This would prove to be Mackey's last turn at the helm, too. It lasted just under a year, ending in September 1942 when his appointment was terminated.

Meanwhile, a short distance outside the city limits of Las Vegas a major event occurred. On April 3, 1941, the El Rancho Vegas Hotel and Casino opened, making it the first resort on what would become the world-famous Las Vegas Strip. Las Vegas' population continued to swell, to 8,500.

Dave Mackey died on January 6, 1944.

Don Borax

Born in Boston, Massachusetts, in 1896, Don Borax took over the department in October 1942. Prior to that, he served in World War I and worked as a stuntman in Hollywood, appearing in several western movies. He next hired on with the Los Angeles Police Department. Six years later, he moved to Nevada and took a job with the Clark County Sheriff's Department.

While Borax was running the department, prostitution became one of the more troublesome problems facing the LVPD. Initially, Borax kept a close watch on the "prostitute line." Whenever one of the prostitutes came in to speak with him, Borax ordered her finger-printed and photographed. He then sent her to a doctor to be examined. He kept track of the 100 or so girls and their locations.

However, with the country in the grip of World War II, the military soon ordered the closure of Block 16 and other houses of prostitution in order to protect its personnel at the Las Vegas Aerial Bombing and Gunnery School located on a huge tract of land north of town. Unfortunately, with the madams forced to close their doors, streetwalkers and venereal disease became a concern; attacks on prostitutes also increased. But with all the unattached young men in town, the world's oldest profession flourished.

Late in 1942, Chief Borax suffered multiple leg fractures when he was involved in thwarting an

Don Borax

escape attempt from the jail. As a result of those injuries, he was forced to take a temporary retirement. Although he later returned to work as an Inspector, his days as Chief of Police were over.

Following his service with the LVPD, Borax continued in law enforcement for a time, working as a Deputy United States Marshal. He later opened a variety store at 500 South Main Street, then took on the job of Chief of Security at the Desert Inn Hotel. In his later years, he worked as a host at the Desert Inn. A dining room at the hotel, the Borax Room, was named in his honor.

> In 1943, during Harry Miller's first year in office, three weddings of note took place in Vegas. Dinah Shore married George Montgomery, Tommy Dorsey tied the knot with Pat Dane, and Betty Grable exchanged vows with Harry James.

Harry Miller

Harry Miller and George Thompson

In 1943, Harry Miller was appointed to replace Don Borax. Born in Bakersfield, California, in 1888, Miller moved to Las Vegas in 1928. After becoming a prominent realtor and operating several hotels, he joined the LVPD in 1935. He served as Assistant Chief of Police before being tapped for the top position.

By 1945, Miller had determined that the job was too political for his liking. He resigned in August, becoming the first Las Vegas Chief of Police to leave the position on his own accord. He later joined the Clark County Sheriff's Department as a civil deputy and subsequently became the first president of the Vegas Valley Water District.

Harry Miller passed on in 1958.

Another Californian, George Thompson, was appointed as the temporary replacement for Miller on September 7, 1945. Born in 1907, Thompson joined the LVPD in 1936 and attained the rank of Captain in 1942. His term as temporary chief was supposed to last only three months, expiring on December 31. However, his performance must have been satisfactory, because he retained the position until 1947.

After stepping down from the top spot, he remained with the department, retiring as Inspector of Police in 1962.

George Thompson

Post-war Las Vegas

In 1946, the City of Las Vegas made its first attempt to annex the Strip and the tax revenues that would come with it. That effort was rebuffed by the organized efforts of hotel operators and citizens who preferred the code and tax structure of Clark County. The post-war boom exploded Las Vegas' population, which stood at 40,000 in 1946.

Also in 1946, an up-and-

Las Vegas Police Department—1943

coming singer and actor made an appearance in Vegas as Grand Marshal of Helldorado Days. Frank Sinatra was greeted by an enthusiastic Fremont Street crowd estimated at 50,000. That night he performed before a packed house at the War Memorial Auditorium. That was the first, but by no means the last, time Sinatra visited Vegas.

In December of the same year, the Las Vegas Police Protective Association was incorporated as a nonprofit organization. Its membership consisted of regularly employed police officers of the City of Las Vegas. The goal of the PPA was to provide benefits to its members, with special emphasis on assistance for the widows and children of deceased officers.

Horner, Malburg, Wells, and Maxwell

On December 5, 1947, Luther Horner was appointed Acting Police Chief. Born in Dial, Texas, in 1906, Horner arrived in Las Vegas in 1931. He owned and operated a grocery store until being hired as a police officer in 1940. He served for one year before joining the security staff of Basic Magnesium Incorporated, the huge metal-processing factory complex built for the war effort in newly established Henderson in southeast Las Vegas Valley. He rejoined the Las Vegas Police Department in 1945, when he was appointed as the Superintendent of Identification.

On December 11, just six days after his appointment as chief, Luther Horner was found dead in his home. Although there was some speculation that he had been murdered, his death was officially ruled a suicide. It was determined that Horner had become mentally unbalanced because of a series of unfortunate events that occurred during his brief reign. He allegedly believed that men within the police department were conspiring to discredit him.

Whatever the reason for his death, Luther Horner was not in office long enough to have any major impact on the direction of the department.

San Francisco native Robert

Luther Horner

Malburg was tapped as the new Las Vegas Chief of Police on December 15, 1947, at a salary of $400 per month. Born in 1901, Malburg worked as an embalmer in a funeral home, an LAPD officer, and served in the Navy prior to coming to Las Vegas.

Robert Malburg

Although the Valley was growing and modernizing, Chief Malburg's jurisdiction had only two traffic lights—always on flash—and cowboys still rode their horses into town and tied them to on-street hitching posts while they visited the downtown saloons.

Three major milestones were reached during his two years in office: The first female police officer—Annabelle Plunkett—was sworn in on January 19, 1948; a civil-service system was established to deal with problems of political interference within the police department; and the Record Bureau was streamlined by consolidating all of the department's functions under one alphabetical master index file. The streamlining resulted in police personnel being able to easily access information on all persons who were arrested, wanted, fingerprinted, or mentioned in complaints. Those

Archie Wells

in the file included casino workers, who were now required by county ordinance to be fingerprinted and to provide personal information. Additionally, two new teletype machines were installed.

On December 14, 1949, Chief Malburg resigned and was replaced by LVPD Sergeant Archie Wells.

The Texas native was born in 1913 and moved to Las Vegas in 1942. After serving in the Army in World War II, he joined the department in 1945. On June 1, 1950, Wells' status was changed from Acting Chief to Chief of Police, but he served only one additional month. Archie Wells died in 1986 at age 73.

On July 1, 1950, Jack Maxwell was named the next LVPD Chief of Police. Born in Arizona in 1881, Maxwell spent time working as a plant security chief for the Ford Motor Company in Detroit, Michigan. After that he moved to Montebello, California, where he ran that city's police department

The Blue Room Dies

On August 19, 1947, the *Las Vegas Review-Journal* reported: "After Many Delays, New Modern City Jail Is Opened. Historic Blue Room Dies But Mourners Are Few."

Although the cost of the new police headquarters and jail had risen to $365,000 from the original estimate of $140,000, Las Vegas now had a state-of-the-art facility.

The new building had metal detectors that could find contraband on fully clothed prisoners. Jailers could see every inch of the detention rooms through the bars, out of the reach of the inmates. Isolation cells allowed members of gangs to be separated to prevent them from discussing their alibis. A room for the storage of inmate possessions automatically locked itself if the staff forgot to do it. The only padded cells for hundreds of miles were available for violent prisoners. Police radio communications allowed for instantaneous communication between officers. And a burglar-proof and fireproof safe was provided to store evidence.

The Blue Room—the Las Vegas version of the Black Hole of Calcutta—was no more.

from 1927 to 1948. He came to Las Vegas in 1949 to help reorganize the LVPD.

As the result of an attempted jailbreak during his first week in office, Maxwell introduced a new policy that required jail officers to visit each cell every half-hour to verify that all prisoners were accounted for. Also during his term, the first civil-service test for LVPD officers was held on August 10, 1950.

In 1951, the results of a national survey comparing the salaries of various occupations were released. The cops learned that they were on the bottom of the wage ladder of the occupations listed. The statistics revealed that bricklayers, plumbers, and carpenters made $3, $2.80 and $2.45 per hour, respectively, plus overtime. Police pay was $1.38 for patrolmen and $1.54 for sergeants with no overtime. In addition to the low pay, the officers were responsible for most of their clothing and equipment costs. They were "loaned" breast and hat badges and one uniform; everything else had to be purchased out-of-pocket.

Jack Maxwell retired in 1952 and returned to Montebello. He died on December 11, 1955.

The Roaring '50s

Alexander Kennedy replaced Maxwell on January 18, 1952. Born in Waukegan, Illinois, on July 11, 1914, he first came to Las Vegas in 1941 in conjunction with his military service. After his discharge in 1945, he returned as a permanent resident.

Kennedy was in office on and off for four years. Quitting in 1953 to accept the position of Acting Las Vegas City Manager, he returned, then left again, for the same job in 1955. He returned and then accepted the City Manager position on a permanent basis in 1956. Each time he left, Kennedy was replaced by George Allen.

Kennedy started out in 1952 earning a salary of $503 per month and heading a staff of 64. By Febru-

Alexander Kennedy

ary 1954, the department had grown to a total of 91 personnel: one chief, 67 officers, 4 lieutenants, and 19 civilians. The Detective Bureau had a Chief of Detectives, eight detectives, and a stenographer. The Identification Bureau had equipment that included a microscope for doing bullet comparisons, a compound microscope for testing physical evidence, and a slide projector.

George Allen

Alexander Kennedy died in 1961.

George Allen began his second term as Chief of Police in June 1955. Born in Media, Pennsylvania, in 1915, Allen came to Las Vegas while in the U.S. Air Force in 1943. He was hired by the LVPD in 1946 and attained the rank of Lieutenant in 1948. After again being briefly replaced by Alexander Kennedy, Allen served as Chief until being relieved by the City Manager's Office in May 1956 for medical reasons.

George Allen served as Assistant Chief in 1960 and as Assistant Sheriff when the LVPD merged with the Clark County Sheriff's Department in 1973. Allen retired in 1976 after a 30-year law-enforcement career. He died in June 2001 at the age of 85.

Officers Down

On April 8, 1955, Sergeant Robert F. Dula, Jr. was killed in the line of duty. With just under three years on the job, the 25-year-old worked in the Uniform Division before being transferred to the Detective Bureau. He'd been promoted to Sergeant on January 16, 1954, and was a motorcycle officer at the time of his death.

At 10:50 that night, just 10 minutes before the end of his tour, Sgt. Dula and his partner received a report of an injured citizen lying in the road at the intersection of Las Vegas Boulevard and Fremont Street. Riding their motorcycles toward the scene with lights and sirens on, Sgt. Dula was struck by a vehicle operated by two juveniles at Twelfth and Fremont. The juveniles fled the scene without stopping. Sgt. Dula's motorcycle went out of control and struck two other vehicles as it careened more than 100 feet from the point of impact. Critically injured, Sgt. Dula was rushed to a hospital, but died two hours later. A wife and two young children survived him.

Also in 1955, on November 4, the police were notified of a burglary involving the theft of $300 in coins, a pellet gun, and a .22 revolver. Later that day, the police were called to a down-town hotel where a maid had found a large number of coins in a guest's room. The guest, who turned out to be a 25-year-old convicted felon, was not in when the officers arrived, but the coins and other evidence found in the room tied the felon to the burglary. Before leaving, the cops advised the desk clerk to notify them as soon as the suspect returned.

At 2:42 p.m., the clerk called the station and reported that the suspect was back in his room; two units were dispatched to the scene.

The first officer to arrive was Wilbur Eugene McGee. Although he'd been on the job only 17 months, the 33-year-old had received several commendations for arrests of wanted felons. Upon entering the hotel, McGee went to the suspect's room, where he placed him under arrest. As

**Robert F. Dula, Jr.
(left)**

**Wilbur E. McGee
(below)**

The Strip Rises

During the 1950s, the City of Las Vegas wasn't the only place experiencing dramatic growth. In the county, the Strip saw the arrival of the Desert Inn in 1950. In 1952, the Sahara and Sands opened, becoming the Strip's sixth and seventh resorts. They were followed in 1955 by the Riviera and the Dunes, the Hacienda in 1956, and the Tropicana in 1957. The Stardust came on the scene in 1958.

Although it was not on the Strip, the Moulin Rouge hotel and casino opened on West Bonanza Road in 1955. At a time when black entertainers had to live off-premises while performing at Strip hotels and black patrons were generally not welcome at Strip properties, the Moulin Rouge was built to accommodate the growing black population and was frequented by all races.

On the entertainment front, Frank Sinatra began a long-term relationship with the Sands and he and his friends, known as the Rat Pack, ruled the Strip. Celebrity weddings included Rita Hayworth and Dick Haymes in 1953, Kirk Douglas and Ann Buydens in 1954, Joan Crawford and Alfred Steele in 1955, and Paul Newman and Joanne Woodward in 1958. The first topless showgirls appeared on the Strip in 1957, when the Dunes opened *Minsky's Follies*.

Starting in the '50s, casino lounge shows provided entertainment that customers could enjoy for the price of a drink. Lounge shows became major attractions in their own right and produced such names as Don Rickles, Buddy Hackett, Shecky Greene, Alan King, and Louis Prima and Keely Smith.

Vegas was drawing former, current, and future stars. And the stars were drawing the tourists.

McGee began to apply handcuffs, the suspect pulled a gun from his waistband and shot the lawman four times. When the backup unit arrived a few seconds later, Officer McGee lay dead on the floor, his gun missing. The suspect was arrested a short time later, still possessing McGee's weapon.

Officer Wilbur McGee was survived by his wife.

A Popular Chief Takes a Fall

In May 1956, Ray Sheffer was appointed the next LVPD Chief of Police. Born in Clarksville, Arkansas, in 1924, Sheffer moved to Las Vegas after his discharge from the Navy at the end of World War II. He was hired by the LVPD in 1948 and quickly rose through the ranks.

In 1957, Sheffer implemented the LVPD Rehabilitation Farm program for sentenced misdemeanants. In 1959, the agency's first Police Academy was held and the first K-9 units appeared. All were considered major achievements that moved the department forward.

In 1959 during Sheffer's term, LVPD officers arrested two of the most notorious criminals in the country at the time. Perry Smith and Richard Hickock were wanted for the November murders of the Herbert Clutter family in Kansas. These crimes resulted in the Truman Capote book, *In Cold Blood*.

The Las Vegas cops had received word that the two suspected killers were heading in their direc-

Ray Sheffer

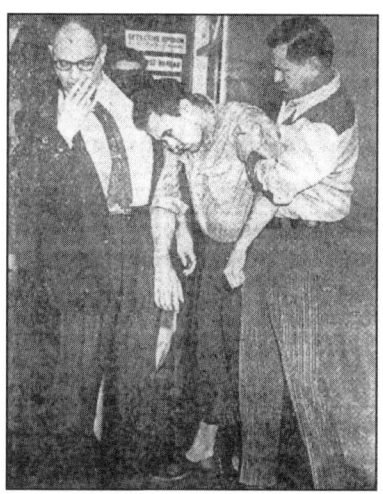

In Cold Blood **killer collapses as he's taken into custody by Las Vegas police.**

tion in a stolen car. A little after 5 p.m. on December 30, the hot 1956 Chevrolet was spotted at the train station. The pair were taken into custody without incident. They were subsequently sent back to Kansas where they were tried, convicted, and sentenced to death. Both men were hung on April 14, 1965.

But there were problems under Sheffer's watch, too. A burglary ring involving police officers was uncovered, setting off a scandal that eventually caused Sheffer's downfall.

A police officer admitted to the crime and was fired, but he was never prosecuted because detectives couldn't independently prove a case against him. However, even though neither man had a role in the burglaries, Chief Sheffer and former Chief Alexander Kennedy were indicted by a grand-jury in August 1960 for "willful omission of duty," alleging that they had failed to act against a burglary ring operating during both of their administrations. The two men were arrested by the Clark County Sheriff's Department on August 23. Sheffer resigned the same day.

The charges were subsequently dismissed, but the damage to Sheffer's career had already been done. The otherwise popular Chief was not reinstated.

Wilbur E. McGee
(fallen officer)

Leo Kuykendall

More Politics in the Chief's Office

The next man to occupy the Chief of Police's office was Leo Kuykendall. Born in Oklahoma, he came to Las Vegas in 1954 as a Special Agent in the local FBI office. By 1960, he was the Assistant Special Agent in charge of that office and had attained a total of 21 years of FBI service. On November 16 of that year, he was appointed to the Chief's position. Receiving a salary of $13,500 per year, he was the highest paid Chief in LVPD history.

Kuykendall's frequent run-ins with the city personnel director exhibited his resistance to City Hall pressures concerning the operation of his department. Although the reason was never made public, the City Councilors cast a no-confidence vote against Kuykendall on November 27, 1964; he was asked to resign or be fired.

Kuykendall maintained that he had done nothing wrong, but rumors were swirling that in addition to friction with City Hall, he had formed a spy network within the department that kept tabs on internal problems and gathered evidence against fellow officers.

Whatever the real reasons, Leo Kuykendall resigned that same day. He subsequently took a position with Binion's Horseshoe Hotel and later returned to Oklahoma, where he passed away in 1999.

The Last Decade of the LVPD

Loren Bunker, a native Nevadan, was born in 1910. He began his law-enforcement career with the LVPD in 1940. In 1956 he was named Chief of Police of the North Las Vegas Police Department; from there he moved on to become the Undersheriff for the Clark County Sheriff's Department. From that position he was picked to become the LVPD Chief of Police on November 27, 1964. He remained in that capacity until his retirement in 1968.

During Bunker's tenure, a new jail opened on the second floor of the City Hall complex. Also, the efficiency of the department was enhanced dramatically. For example, it hooked up to the new FBI Crime Center in Washington. Fifteen seconds after the LVPD teletyped the name or license-plate number of a stopped motorist or suspect, the FBI would respond as to whether the vehicle or person was wanted. Several large books maintained locally were cross-indexed and provided for rapid access to license and registration information and

Loren Bunker

The 1960s saw continued news from the burgeoning entertainment industry. In August 1960, the movie *Ocean's Eleven*, starring Frank Sinatra and the Rat Pack, premiered. Set in Vegas, the plot involved a group of former soldiers robbing several casinos simultaneously. Sinatra got additional headlines in 1966 when he married Mia Farrow at the Sands.

Other famous couplings of the '60s included Cary Grant and Dyan Cannon in 1965, Xavier Cougat and Charo in '66, Elvis Presley and Priscilla Beaulieu the following year, and Wayne Newton and Elaine Okamura in 1968.

---

records of violations. A confidential file was kept on persons who were considered to be "suspicious," but had no criminal record. A special switch connected the LVPD dispatcher with the Clark County Sheriff's Department and all police field units.

On June 1, 1968, after several months of rumors of stepping down, Chief Bunker officially retired. On the same day his replacement was named: N. "Pete" Witcher.

Witcher was born in Quitaque, Texas, in 1917. His family moved to California, where the 23-year-old hired on with the Monterey County Sheriff's Department. After reaching the rank of Captain with that agency, he moved to Las Vegas in 1954. He joined the Clark County Sheriff's Department, resigning a year later to become Chief of Security at the Dunes Hotel and Casino. He later served in the same capacity at both the New Frontier and the Flamingo.

In 1967, Pete Witcher was recruited to become one of two LVPD Deputy Chiefs. From that position he was promoted to Chief, where he served until 1972. The first police helicopter in Las Vegas was placed into operation during the Witcher administration.

In 1972, Witcher resigned to become Vice President of Corpo-

Pete Witcher

rate Security for Caesars Palace. He passed away in February 2000 at age 82.

The next and last Chief of Police of the LVPD was John Moran. Born in San Fernando, California, in 1922, Moran attended the University of Arizona on an athletic scholarship and became one of the nation's top javelin throwers.

After a tour in the Marine Corps, he moved to Las Vegas in 1947 and joined the police department a year later; he was appointed Chief in 1972.

John Moran was instrumental in creating the July 1, 1973, merger between his agency and the Clark County Sheriff's Department that formed the Las Vegas Metropolitan

John Moran

Police Department. When the new department was formed, he became the first undersheriff and later served 12 years as sheriff.

K-9 and Off-Duty Officers Killed

On October 28, 1966, Officer William Robert Fortye was killed in the line of duty.

Bill Fortye joined the LVPD in 1961; after two years on the job he joined the K-9 Corps. He and his four-footed partner Burgie received numerous commendations for preventing crimes and apprehending criminals.

At 2:20 a.m. on the night of his death, Fortye called in a traffic stop on Highland Drive. Nothing indicated anything out of the ordinary; it appeared to be just another routine stop. Ten minutes later he was dead.

William Fortye with Burgie the police dog

The first officers to arrive on the scene found Officer Fortye lying alongside his patrol car, with Burgie standing faithfully by. Evidence showed that a violent struggle had taken place between Fortye and his assailant, with the suspect gaining control of Fortye's weapon and shooting him three times. Before the killer fled Burgie attacked, ripping his clothing and mauling his hand. The subject was caught a short time later.

Bill Fortye was 32 when he died and was survived by his wife and six-year-old daughter.

Sergeant Paul De Weert joined the LVPD in 1948. He had served as a combat Marine in World War II and survived several shooting incidents during his law-enforcement career. At age 60 he was known as "Pappy" by his fellow officers.

On the evening of October 8, 1967, while Sgt. De Weert was technically off-duty, he encountered an intoxicated individual whom he asked to stop so he could speak with him. A drunken ex-con,

Paul De Weert

who was later apprehended, gunned down the unarmed De Weert at a dark North Las Vegas intersection, just two blocks from the home he shared with his wife and two teenage sons.

2

Clark County Sheriff's Department 1909-1973

The Early Years

On July 1, 1909, amid great fanfare, huge Clark County, still one of the largest counties in the U.S., was carved from even huger Lincoln County in southern Nevada. On July 3, Charles C.

Charles C. Corkhill

Corkhill was appointed to serve as the first Clark County Sheriff until the regular election was held in 1910. Corkhill was a newspaper editor and had no law-enforcement experience. Sam Gay, of Block 16 fame, was appointed as his Chief Deputy.

The two men were opposites in many important ways. Sheriff Corkhill was a moral man who detested rowdiness and had a special dislike for drinking. Sam Gay was an admitted boozer. When he was off duty, Gay would sometimes have a few drinks and celebrate by shooting the lights out at City Hall and on Fremont Street. He and Corkhill clashed frequently.

The final straw for Corkhill came in the summer of 1910. With temperatures in the corrugated jail reaching 117 degrees, Sam Gay removed the prisoners and marched them to Las Vegas Creek. Once there, he chained them loosely to the trees that lined the bank. When Sheriff Corkhill learned that the inmates were beating the heat by lounging in the shade next to the creek, he became incensed and promptly fired Gay.

For Corkhill, this proved to be a serious error in judgment. His former Chief Deputy ran against him in the fall election and the voters overwhelmingly chose the "drinker" over the blue-nose Corkhill.

In 1911, Gay was appointed as the first Las Vegas Chief of Police, holding the Sheriff and Chief of Police positions simultaneously until giving up the LVPD job in 1914.

Sam Gay

Although well-liked generally, Sheriff Gay sometimes offended the more refined ladies of Las Vegas. In 1914, the county constructed a new two-story courthouse facing Second Street and used the old building as City Hall. The former courthouse also held Sam Gay's office, with a library located next to it. On occasion, the ladies visiting the library were subjected to the strong smell of liquor, the rattling of bottles, and the singing of off-color songs coming from Sam's office. The women voiced their concerns, but Sheriff Gay felt that a man had a right to relax and let off steam in his own office. So the women continued to complain and Sam continued to drink.

On October 6, 1917, Sam Gay was removed from office for refusing to arrest one of his deputies. Deputy Joe Keate was an hour late getting to court, where he was an important witness in an ongoing trial. When Keate did show up, the judge was indignant and pointed out that Keate already had a black mark against him for previously pulling his gun in court and threatening to shoot another judge.

Sam spoke up on Keate's behalf and angry words flew across the courtroom between Sam and the judge. When the court finally ordered that Keate be arrested, Sam refused to comply. Sheriff Gay was suspended and subsequently terminated. Deputy Keate was fired outright.

W.B. "Will" Mundy, a Canadian with no law-enforcement experience, who was the manager of the Western Union office, was appointed to replace Sam Gay on the day of Sam's suspension. Mundy resigned as sheriff four weeks later and returned to his job with the telegraph company. As the reason for his resignation, Mundy said that the job was "too hazardous."

Later on, Mundy served for approximately 10 years as a Las Vegas City Councilor. He died in 1949 at the age of 79.

Chicago native Jay Warren Woodard was named as Will Mundy's successor in November 1917. His top priority was to close down the prostitution on Block 16. Unfortunately for Sheriff Woodard, Block 16 was the main source of day-to-day cash in town. The railroad—the largest employer in the area—paid their employees monthly. With the prostitutes out of operation, Block 16 and the cash flow dried up. Local businessmen, who eventually ended up with the money generated from Block 16, went into a panic. They told the Councilors that unless things quickly returned to normal, they would see to it that all current officeholders were ousted. The "girls" were back in business the day after the ultimatum was delivered.

Not long afterward, the people of Las Vegas and Clark County let it be known that they wanted Sam Gay back as their chief lawman. He was reelected in the fall

W.B. Mundy

Jay Warren Woodard (right)

of 1918, a year after being thrown out of office.

Jay Woodard returned to running the Chevrolet dealership from where he had come. He passed on in September 1944 at the age of 70.

Sam Gay went on to serve another 12 years as Sheriff of Clark County. A couple of years before leaving office, a newspaper article quoted from one of Sam's letters to the voters. The November 3, 1928, *Illustrated Daily News* said in part:

"Thirty-two of the last thirty-four men that were sent from Clark County to the Nevada State Prison had pleaded guilty, saving the taxpayers the expense of thirty-two jury trials. I have arrested or caused the arrest in 95 percent of all felony crimes committed in Clark County in the last 15 years. I have arrested scores of felony prisoners for other states. I have been a peace officer in California and Nevada for 25 years and never lost a prisoner; never shot a man; never hit a man on the head with a gun; always gave everybody a square deal in or out of jail.

"From 1905 to 1910 Las Vegas was a rough and tumble Western town. Five dead men for breakfast one Sunday morning and ten men wounded; the boys put on a show that would make Bill Hart ashamed of himself. Yes, my friends, I had a man's job here from 1905 to 1910 and the people must have approved or they wouldn't have elected me sheriff in 1910."

When Sam announced his retirement in 1930, the 70-year-old cited the following as the reason for his decision:

"Too many crooks coming to Las Vegas, [and] now they're going to build Boulder Dam. I've dealt with honest men so long I wouldn't know how to act around crooks. I'm used to tough hombres who shot each other up once in a while. I'm used to gunfights. But I ain't much good running down racketeers. My notion is too old-fashioned. You can't deal with these new gunmen with a single-action .45. Need a machine gun. I'm too old to learn to run one, so I quit."

Sam Gay died on August 24, 1932, at the age of 72.

But The Story Doesn't End There

Joe Keate, the fired deputy whom Gay refused to arrest, was elected sheriff in November 1930. Keate was born in St. George, Utah, in 1880. He joined the Clark County Sheriff's Department under Sam Gay and later moved on to the Las Vegas Police Department. He served his term as Sheriff during one of the most hectic times in the history of the county—the building of Hoover Dam.

Upon assuming office, Keate

Joe Keate

retained two deputies from Sam Gay's administration and appointed a man named Albert Calkins to work out of Searchlight, a mining settlement 60 miles south of Las Vegas.

In 1932, the Clark County Sheriff's Department had the distinction of having the youngest full-fledged female deputy sheriff in Nevada. At 21, Marjorie Goodwin had the authority to issue licenses and permits handled by the CCSD.

After serving almost six years, Joe Keate was removed from office for malfeasance. The action was the result of a determination by a judge in Ely, who disagreed with Keate's decision to release a prisoner from the county jail who had served only five days of a 15-day sentence for drunk driving.

After leaving the Sheriff's job, Keate worked for many years as a special investigator for several downtown casinos. He died in 1948 at the age of 68.

On September 26, 1936, Bill Mott, Joe Keate's undersheriff, was appointed to replace his ousted boss. The Utah native was born on September 4, 1883, and moved to Las Vegas in 1921. He worked on the Union Pacific Railroad and for the Pacific Fruit Express Company until Keate selected him as undersheriff in 1931.

With only a few weeks in office, Mott had to face election that November to determine who would fill the two remaining years of Joe Keate's term. His challenger was M.E. "Gene" Ward. When the 6,240 ballots were tallied, Ward won by a total of 36 votes.

Gene Ward was born in Morenci, Michigan, in 1888. He moved to Las Vegas in 1918 and opened the first of his three

Bill Mott

food markets. He could be observed regularly in the small town delivering groceries door-to-door. The prominent merchant founded the famed Helldorado Parade in 1934.

Ward served as Clark County Sheriff until 1943 and then as a Justice of the Peace. He later bought property in Pittman—now Henderson—and operated a casino there for several years.

Gene Ward passed away at the age of 76 in 1964.

Gene Ward

Glen Jones

Born in Overton, Nevada, in 1910, Glen C. Jones began his law-enforcement career with the CCSD in 1935. He rose through the ranks, served as undersheriff to Gene Ward, and was elected Clark County Sheriff in November of 1942.

The department installed a new teletype system in 1945. Leased through the California Department of Justice, it was the only one of its kind in Las Vegas and operated around the clock. The hookup included motor-vehicle registration

Glen Jones

centers, which greatly improved the ability to trace stolen vehicles and those in which fugitives, or wanted persons, were traveling.

In March 1947, the formation of the 50-horsemen Clark County Mounted Posse was announced. That December, fingerprinting of certain Clark County casino employees began. Employees filed personal applications with the CCSD, then appeared at the headquarters on South Third Street for fingerprinting. Before leaving, the applicant received an identification card personally signed by Sheriff Jones.

In March 1948 a Flying Posse was formed as part of the new Aero Squadron. Planes were used for manhunts, rescues, and as transport for public officials. If, during a rescue operation, a plane couldn't land, the crew would drop necessary supplies and equipment to the distressed party by parachute.

During the same year, the radio-communication system was expanded and a master index file was implemented. This file contained information about anyone in the county who had been involved in any accident, crime, or unusual occurrence and could be accessed within a few minutes.

On May 23, 1949, Sheriff Jones was ordered by the County Commissioners to terminate five deputies due to a lack of funds; at that time the department was $12,910 over budget. The cuts were made, forcing the remaining 22 personnel to work 12-hour days with no vacations. A few months later, a grand jury complained about a lack of uniforms for deputies and crowded jail conditions; it also recommended that deputies receive law-enforcement training.

Sheriff Jones explained that deputy sheriffs received a salary of $250 per month for working six days a week, between nine and 14 hours per day. Uniforms cost $50

Clark County Sheriff's Department—circa 1940s

each and the deputies had to buy at least four in a year. He was hoping to get the County Commissioners to pay for the uniforms.

As for the jail, Jones admitted that the living conditions were not the best, but added that the facility had been built 40 years earlier with a capacity for only 20 inmates. The jail was obsolete by 1950 standards.

In May 1950, the Henderson Substation was moved from the outskirts of town to Market Street, next to the Chamber of Commerce building. That station closed in 1953 and the City of Henderson took over its own police functions at that time. Three of the seven men who had been assigned to Henderson were brought into the Las Vegas office, increasing the patrolling available. A new night patrol was added, working from 8 p.m. until 4 a.m. and covering the Paradise Valley area, the Strip, and unincorporated highway towns such as Whitney.

The Roaring '50s

In November 1952, a new $18,000 FM radio system replaced the 1946 vintage AM system. An antenna on Sunrise Mountain enabled communication between two or more patrol cars, providing the units were less than 25 miles apart. All 12 of the Sheriff's Department cars were equipped with transmitters and receivers; Palm Mortuary was also hooked in so they could be dispatched to accident scenes.

In January 1953, the Clark County Sheriff's Mounted Posse went to Washington, D.C., to participate in the inaugural parade of Dwight D. Eisenhower. Located in the center of the procession, the finely clad posse members threw silver dollars to the crowd along the parade route. It was the first time ever that a Clark County organization represented Nevada in an inaugural parade.

Sheriff Jones was defeated in the 1954 election by W.E. "Butch"

Butch Leypoldt

Two Deputies Killed

On December 26, 1950 Deputy Winnie Hansen and his partner, William Wolf, were driving on Boulder Highway when they observed a vehicle being operated erratically. They pulled the car over near the intersection of East Charleston Boulevard. The deputies and the other driver exited their vehicles.

It was quickly determined that the erratic driving was the result of a faulty brake line. As the three men stood talking, they observed another vehicle heading directly for them. Deputy Wolf grabbed the driver and pulled him clear of the oncoming car. Deputy Hansen wasn't able to get out of the way. He was transported to the hospital where he died from his injuries. The driver whose vehicle struck Deputy Hansen was arrested and later convicted of vehicular manslaughter.

George Hart

Winnie Hansen was 56 at the time of his death.

On November 12, 1957 Deputy George Hart died at age 40 as the result of injuries sustained in the line of duty on October 25. Deputy Hart was booking a drunken prisoner he'd arrested when the subject struck him in the stomach area. Hart fought for his life for more than two weeks before succumbing to complications resulting from the assault.

George Hart had joined the CCSD on July 5, 1956, little more than a year before his untimely death. He left behind a wife and five children.

Leypoldt. Glen Jones passed away in 1983 at the age of 73.

Butch Leypoldt

Butch Leypoldt was born in Omaha, Nebraska, in 1914. He moved to Las Vegas in 1938 with his two brothers to operate a pair of gasoline stations. In 1941 he was hired by the LVPD and began his law-enforcement career, interrupted by service during World War II. After being discharged from the military, Leypoldt returned to Las Vegas and hired on with the Clark County Sheriff's Department.

Upon taking office in 1955,

Sheriff Leypoldt changed shift hours. The day shift ran from 10 a.m. to 6 p.m.; swing shift hours were 6 p.m. to 2 a.m.; a combination of swing and graveyard personnel covered the county between 8 p.m. and 4 a.m., and the graveyard shift was from 2 a.m. until 10 a.m. Three patrol cars were out on all shifts; there was one officer per car on the day shift, while the night shifts operated with two-man crews.

To combat the rising drug problem, Leypoldt issued an advisory to Clark County parents. He asked them to be observant of their children when arriving home at night, and to watch for:

"… a smell of burnt rope on the breath, or if their eyes present a widely dilated, fixed staring pupil with the whites severely bloodshot and if the foregoing symptoms are accompanied by the following physiological reactions: The child being hilarious, hysterical, weeping,

laughing or speaking rapidly in loud tones." If any of theses conditions existed, the parents were told to contact the CCSD immediately, regardless of the time of day.

In 1961, during his second

First Female Captain

Helen Anne Moore was the first female in the CCSD to hold the title of Captain. She was promoted by Sheriff Leypoldt on August 6, 1960.

Moore was born in Canada in 1917. She moved to Las Vegas in 1946 and became a naturalized citizen of the United States. After working at the Clark County Recorders Office, she was commissioned as a deputy sheriff on February 7, 1951. She rose through the ranks and held the position of Chief Civil Deputy prior to her promotion.

term, Sheriff Leypoldt resigned when he was selected by Governor Grant Sawyer to serve on the Gaming Control Board. He passed away in May 1990 at age 75.

In 1957, the CCSD employed 52 deputies, 45 of whom were assigned to the Criminal Division and 7 to the Civil Division. Its jurisdiction covered a land area of more than 8,500 square miles. This territory included the Strip with its 13 resorts and 47 smaller hotels and motels. In total, the county contained 51 hotels and 250 motels. One of the fastest-growing population areas in the United States even back then, Clark County had 98,000 residents and 55,000 automobiles.

The Lamb Era Begins

The resignation of Sheriff Leypoldt opened the way for the emergence of a man who would serve as sheriff for the next 17 years: Ralph Lamb. In 1961 he was appointed to fill Leypoldt's unfinished term. Ironically, Lamb had opposed the same Leypoldt in the 1958 election and lost. In 1963 he was elected to the Sheriff's position outright.

Ralph Lamb was born in the Mormon farming community of Alamo, Nevada, on April 10, 1927. The Lambs were a ranching family, and although he lost both his grandfather and father to accidents involving horses, Ralph himself became an avid horseman. One of 11 children, he went straight from high school into the Army to serve in the final year of World War II. He hired on with the CCSD in 1948 and resigned in 1955 to operate a private detective agency for the next six years. His main client dur-

ing that time was none other than Howard Hughes, who required that all communications between them be handled via a pay phone.

Lamb returned to a department that had grown to 350 employees. For nearly two decades he led it through a period of unprecedented growth and modernization, including its consolidation with the Las Vegas Police Department to form the Las Vegas Metropolitan Police Department.

Among the many firsts in Sheriff Lamb's early years: In January 1962, the department hired its first female radio dispatcher, Suletta Ainley; in February 1963, a 24-hour-a-day substation was opened at the new Clark County Airport; and in 1964 helmets were issued to patrol offices. Carried in the trunks of their cars, the helmets were utilized during civil disturbances rather than as protection against injury during an automobile accident.

On August 20, 1964, the British rock group, the Beatles, appeared at the Las Vegas Convention Center. Two days before the event, deputies reported to the parking lot of that facility for extensive training in crowd and riot control. The cops split into two squadrons, one representing the "good guys," and the other playing the part of "Beatle-maniacs." The "bad guys" shouted insults and jeered at the "fuzz." The officers brandished their clubs and waded into the unruly crowd, practicing tactics designed to split the crowd and force the fans back.

The drills were intended to be realistic, and they were. During the scuffles, uniforms were damaged, including that of one officer who literally had the seat ripped out of his pants. With emotions running high and minor injuries mounting, the sergeant in charge dismissed the troops after an hour into the slugfest. Though he wasn't satisfied with their performance, he was afraid that if he continued the train-

Ralph Lamb

ing, he wouldn't have enough of a crew fit for duty to work the actual concert.

A new substation was opened in East Las Vegas in 1964. In 1965, under the Resident Officer program, a resident facility was opened in Overton; in 1967, a similar post was established in Laughlin. By the end of the 1960s, resident stations were located throughout far-flung Clark County, including in Searchlight, Fort Mojave, Mt. Charleston, Indian Springs, and Mesquite.

A major advance in record-keeping occurred in 1968 with the introduction of SCOPE—Shared Computer Operations for Protection and Enforcement. The online computerized master-name index provided around-the-clock information on individuals and businesses. Entries that had formerly been made via punch card could now be done using a video terminal. In 1971, Ralph Lamb received a $100,000 federal grant to update the SCOPE system and tie it in with the computers in the Clark County Courthouse.

In 1970, Sheriff Lamb had to

intervene in a confrontation involving singer Frank Sinatra and a casino executive. The performer was engaged in an ongoing battle with the casino over his casino credit limit. On this particular occasion, the altercation became quite heated and the executive pulled a gun on Sinatra. After investigating, Lamb threatened to arrest the singer and throw him in jail. The matter was resolved without further incident.

The "mother of all changes" was still ahead, however. In late 1968, actions commenced that would change the face of law enforcement in Clark County forever.

The Road To Consolidation

In December 1968, the Las Vegas Police Department and the Clark County Sheriff's Department formed a study team to examine the feasibility of consolidating their public-safety services. At that time, the police and sheriff's departments were the two largest police agencies in Nevada, each having approximately 500 personnel, both sworn and civilian. The LVPD jurisdiction comprised about 53 square miles, while the CCSD was responsible for more than 8,000 square miles of unincorporated territory. Its area covered from California on the south and west to the Arizona border on the east and the Utah and Lincoln County borders on the north.

Independent of this law-enforcement initiative, the respective governments bickered over whether or not to incorporate urbanized areas of the county into the city. Las Vegas argued that it was better able to provide urban services and that the county should limit itself to governing rural areas. If successful, the City of Las Vegas would gobble up the Strip and its lucrative tax revenues. The County Board of Commissioners vigorously opposed the plan.

The County Commissioners authorized the Public Administration Service of Chicago, Illinois, to conduct a study of local government and make recommendations for streamlining the services they provided. The PAS completed its work and made recommendations, many of which favored Clark County. However, Las Vegas officials believed that the report was biased and no action was taken.

The 1969 session of the Nevada Legislature made an effort to pass a law that would have abolished the city charters of Las Vegas and North Las Vegas, creating a single metropolitan government.

If established, the new government entity would annex the previously discussed urbanized areas of Clark County. Governor Mike O'Callaghan vetoed assembly Bill 783 due to strong opposition from local elected officials.

The 1971 legislative session made another attempt to consolidate local government. The Local Government Study Committee held public hearings to determine how local government might be improved. On December 15 of that year, the Committee directed that the City of Las Vegas and the County Commissioners appoint members of their law-enforcement departments to determine those areas of each agency that could be consolidated. Specifically targeted were Records, Criminalistics, Detention, and Communications.

On January 28, 1972, the first meeting of the Law Enforcement Study Committee was held. It consisted of nine members, including three officers of the CCSD and four from the LVPD. Among the LVPD representatives were Captain Larry Ketzenberger and Deputy Chief Amos Elliott, Jr.; Chief Deputy Ray Gubser was one of the CCSD representatives.

In 2002, Amos Elliot remembered his service on the Committee quite clearly.

"When I first studied the possibility of consolidation in 1968 and saw the many potential benefits, I knew it was the only way to go," Elliot recalled. "There was too much duplication and confusion. Sometimes there were debates over whose jurisdiction an incident occurred in. These situations weren't conducive to efficiently serving the public."

The crooks also made it a point to know where each agency's turf started and ended. They knew that they could sometimes escape arrest by simply crossing a street into the other department's territory.

Larry Ketzenberger, too, was a

Consolidation Staff

supporter of consolidation. In the text of a 1974 speech he gave to a meeting of the National Sheriff's Association, he provided insights into the consolidation process and the concerns the Law Enforcement Study Committee had to confront.

"The members of the two departments sat across the table from one another—eyeing each other warily. Very little was accomplished during the first few meetings because each side mistrusted the motives of the other.

"It became apparent to the majority of the members that the only practical way to merge any of the functions was to work toward a total merger of both departments. The Committee first worked on the administrative relationships based on the philosophy that it would be senseless to work out the details for merging the operating divisions without the concurrence of the administrative structure. It might be properly said that much negotiation went on within the Committee, a give and take on both sides. There was agreement that an elected, rather than an appointed, official should be in charge of the new department, someone less likely to be influenced by outside political pressure. The city officers were in favor of retaining civil service protection while some of the county officers did not like the connotation that the term civil service provided. These officers felt that the merit system, which was used by the Sheriff's Department, provided a better flavor than civil service. After evaluating the merits of the many positions, the Committee was able to recommend a merger of the two entities in a manner which they felt would be feasible and which would ultimately give the citizens of Clark County more efficient law enforcement."

Captain Ketzenberger also mentioned an added momentum for prompt attention to the consolidation issue: "It should be noted that during the meetings being held by the Law Enforcement Study Committee, we were under the understanding and belief that the 1973 Legislature would require some form of merger or consolidation and, had it not been for this impetus, it is quite possible that the Committee would not have worked as hard to pound out recommendations which would provide for a total merger of the two departments."

In other words, the police officers were convinced that if they didn't work quickly to set up their own merger plans, the politicians in Carson City would.

On October 5, 1972, the Committee submitted a formal report to the City of Las Vegas and the Clark County Commissioners for their approval. The report was accepted in its entirety.

The merger plan called for a new agency to be called the Las Vegas Metropolitan Police Department to be established, and the two existing departments to be abolished. The chief law-enforcement officer for the new department would be the elected Sheriff of Clark County. The Chief of Police of the Las Vegas Police Department would become the Undersheriff and the former Assistant Chief of Police and the Undersheriff designated as Assistant Sheriffs. All other appointive staff would remain in their respective positions and use the title of Deputy Chief. A Police Commission comprised of city and county officials would be created and have the authority for approval of the department's budget.

The plan further provided that no personnel, sworn or civilian, would suffer any loss in pay, pension, fringe, or other job benefits. In fact, former Las Vegas officers would receive an immediate pay increase up to the higher Sheriff's Department wage. In turn, Clark County employees gained better-defined job protection under Civil Service Rules. The Sheriff's Policy Manual would provide the governing rules and regulations, while the Las Vegas Police Department's Civil Service Rules would be adopted for the new department. The Protective Associations of both departments would merge to represent the officers of "Metro."

The plan was submitted to the Legislature in January 1973. Members of the Law Enforcement Study Committee monitored the progress of the legislation to make sure the bill was passed as intended.

On April 16, an emergency meeting of the Committee was held in Sheriff Lamb's office. Word had been received that some County Commissioners were attempting to introduce amendments that would alter the consolidation bill by changing the authority of the Police Commission to an advisory role only. The next day, five members of the Committee flew to Carson City to protest the proposed change. Their efforts were successful and the bill was passed as written. Effective July 1, 1973, the Las Vegas Police Department and the Clark County Sheriff's Department ceased to exist and the Las Vegas Metropolitan Police Department came into being.

3

Las Vegas Metropolitan Police Department 1973-Present

Introduction

As dawn broke over the Las Vegas Valley on July 1, 1973, Clark County had become home to the largest police agency in Nevada, responsible for law enforcement in the City of Las Vegas and all unincorporated areas of the county. However, a number of problems existed, in spite of the best efforts of the Law Enforcement Study Committee.

Although not immediately brought to light, financial problems loomed. When the enabling legislation was passed, no funds were granted to pay for the additional costs associated with the consolidation. For example, former city employees had not only received a base salary increase, they would now be paid time-and-a-half for overtime, plus increased hazardous-duty pay and uniform allowances. It was estimated that between July 1, 1973, and June 30, 1974, the extra costs for former city personnel would be approximately $290,000.

Sheriff's employees had negotiated a salary increase prior to the merger amounting to $206,000 for the same period. The costs for achieving uniformity through the standardization of uniforms, badges, caps, leather gear, service weapons, and vehicles was estimated at another $284,000. This meant a budget shortfall of approximately $750,000 by June 30, 1974. On the bright side, many of these costs were one time in nature and future budgets would provide the necessary funding levels.

Unlike the money issues, personnel and equipment problems

were visible from the first day. At the initial briefings, officers were arrayed in the uniforms of their former departments and tended not to mix with each other. The city cops wore .38s, while their county brothers carried 9mms. When putting together the consolidation plan, the Committee had designed a new uniform for Metro. After consolidation, though, Undersheriff John Moran vetoed the new uniform as a cost-cutting measure. He decided that because the county uniform was better looking than the city's, it would be the uniform of the new department.

Metro's official weapon would be the Sheriff's Department 9mm. Deputy Chief Amos Elliott had argued for acquisition of .45 semi-automatics. The Committee rejected his proposal in a close vote in favor of the 9mm. One of the reasons for the decision was financial: the deputies were already equipped with that weapon and only the former city cops would have to be supplied with the new guns. It had also been decided that new police cars would be introduced. The proposed color scheme of desert tan and white was discarded when it soon became obvious that these

"Routine" Traffic Stop Turns Deadly

On February 22, 1978 Traffic Officer James Richard Rogan made a "routine" traffic stop on Paradise Road. Unbeknown to him, the driver of the vehicle was wanted for a series of crimes in Alaska. As the eight-year veteran was writing a citation, the fugitive became fearful that Rogan had discovered his identity. The suspect shot the officer with a semi-automatic handgun, dropping him to the pavement. The gunman then emptied his weapon into the fallen Rogan.

The suspect was found the next morning after an all-night house-to-house search. Refusing to surrender, he was killed by his victim's colleagues.

James Rogan died at the age of 41, leaving behind a wife and six children. In 1998, his son James was hired by Metro as a police officer and is currently following in his father's footsteps.

vehicles were not being recognized as police cars. Those vehicles were quickly repainted to the "black and whites" formerly used by the county.

However, none of those equipment changes were in place on July 1. In addition to looking different and driving different-colored vehicles, the attitudes of many of the officers were negative. Over the years, animosities had developed between the two agencies, particularly among the rank and file. Professional jealousies and personality conflicts were not easily forgotten; in some cases loyalty ran deep. Many people were simply resistant to change and the uncertainty it engendered. A piece of paper generated in Carson City didn't necessarily mean the birth of a cohesive police mega-department.

There were reports of verbal and physical confrontations between the officers. Allegations arose that "secret" briefings were held for the county people after the regular briefing ended. One city cop said that he had left the formal briefing to go on patrol, but left his clipboard in the briefing room. When he returned to retrieve his property, he found a group of county officers receiving additional information. Needless to say, news of these kinds of activities, real or rumor, did little to allay fears or improve morale.

As time passed, the situation improved. By February 1974, uniformity had been achieved; it was no longer possible to tell which department an officer previously worked for simply by looking at him or her, or the vehicle being driven. Tensions between officers lessened, too, and they were now functioning as members of the same team.

Although there were continuing squabbles on the Police Commission about who would pay what percentage of the budget, the actual policing efforts were working as envisioned; the consolidation was a success.

Tactical Unit

In 1974, the Tactical Unit was formed; on February 21, 1975, it used deadly force for the first time. The incident involved an attempted bank robbery that turned into a hostage situation.

At approximately 10:45 that morning, a lone suspect attempted to rob a bank located on the northwest corner of Maryland Parkway and Karen Avenue. Metro officers showed up during the robbery attempt, trapping the suspect and a teller inside the bank. The standoff lasted most of the day. While the FBI was negotiating with the suspect, members of the Tactical Unit deployed around the bank. A sniper took up a position across the street, where he could observe the movements of the suspect.

At 4:30, talks with the robber reached an impasse. The FBI notified the Tactical Unit Commander that the suspect could be taken out if an opportunity presented itself. Shortly thereafter, the suspect appeared near the bank's front door, giving the sniper a clear shot. One round from the marksman's .243 Model 700 Remington passed through the plate-glass door and struck the suspect in the chest. He collapsed and died inside the bank.

Las Vegas Police Cruisers Through the Years

**LVPD Patrol Car
late 1940s
(left)**

**CCSD 1966
Patrol Car**

LVPD 1941 Chevrolet

1980 LVMPD Patrol Car

1974 Dodge Monaco

The hostage was unharmed.

At 2:20 a.m. on November 11, 1975, Metro Officer James Melvin was taken hostage while investigating a crime in progress at the Village Inn Pancake House at 3065 Las Vegas Boulevard South. As Officer Melvin arrived at the scene, suspect Maxwell Gordon exited a store next to the restaurant and got the drop on him. Melvin was taken to the suspect's vehicle where a female accomplice was waiting. Before Gordon could force Melvin into the car, Officers Ron Fisher and Bernie Elvin pulled into the parking lot and confronted him.

Officer Melvin dropped to the pavement to give Fisher and Elvin a clear view of Gordon; as he did, the suspect opened fire with a .45 semi-automatic handgun. During the shootout, Melvin suffered a bullet wound to his left forearm from Gordon's weapon. The suspect was hit multiple times and died as the result of his wounds. Officer Melvin recovered and returned to duty.

This incident marked the first time an on-duty Metro officer was taken hostage and the first time an accomplice, the woman in Melvin's car, was charged with murder under the new Felony Murder Rule.

Jail Woes

A 1975 grand-jury report found that the Central Detention Facility was overcrowded, provided inadequate medical treatment, and was unsanitary, understaffed, and dangerous to the health and lives of the inmates. It determined that these conditions constituted an emergency situation and recommended a new jail be built. The new building should be limited to one- and two-man cells and have a hospital ward, psychiatric-care facilities, exercise, religious, and recreational areas, and extensive security.

These findings were the result of allegations of cruel and unusual punishment made in 1973 by a convicted murderer while he was temporarily held in that facility. Local authorities admitted in federal court that the detention system did have problems and promised to take corrective measures.

Inmates filed an amended complaint in August 1977, charging that they were held in conditions that were oppressive, barbaric, and degrading. They further alleged that their basic rights as citizens and human beings were being violated. In November 1977 inmate attorneys asked that the U.S. Justice Department join the case against Clark County; in February 1978, it did.

On July 19, the county signed a Jail Consent Decree. This document established a committee to study all alternatives to bring the detention system into compliance as soon as possible. Written recommendations had to be submitted by March 9, 1979. On May 27, 1980, Clark County voters passed a bond issue for the new jail and construction began on April 13, 1981.

On September 13, 1984, almost nine years after the grand-jury report, the new 12-story Clark County Detention Center was opened at 330 South Casino Center in downtown Las Vegas. Built at a cost of $55 million, it was designed to hold 852 inmates and was recognized by the American Correctional Association and the American Institute of Architects as an example of a state-of-the-art correctional facility.

The jail was connected to the Clark County Courthouse by a 480-foot tunnel, reducing the need for bus transportation to get inmates to court appearances. It was designed with expansion in mind, which proved to be a very wise decision, given that Clark County was one of the fastest growing areas in the country.

In order to keep pace with the general population growth and proportionate increases in crime, the bed capacity increased to 1,488 by 1999. Unfortunately, the average daily inmate population had reached 2,526. This meant that a number of prisoners had to be farmed out to other facilities. Yet another expansion completed in 2002 brought the maximum inmate capacity at the jail up to 2,860. The situation is under control, at least for the time being.

Operation Switch

In August 1975 the Intelligence Services Division was created, encompassing the Intelligence, Special Investigations, and Task Force Bureaus.

Also, in 1975, a new unit was formed in the Clark County District Attorney's Office. Funded by a Law Enforcement Assistance Administration grant, the Clark County Conspiratorial Crime Prevention Unit was dedicated to combating conspiracy, fraud, and white-collar crime. The unit was made up of 11 people, including a chief, secretary, and nine investigators. It could fund projects involving other agencies, with the caveat that members of the DA's squad had to participate in any such operation. Jack Miller was an investigator with this new unit.

In 1976, the Las Vegas Metropolitan Police Department came up with a unique idea for combating stolen-property crimes. The LVMPD, FBI, and the DA's Office joined forces for Operation Switch, targeting burglars, robbers, and other thieves. It was one of the first major law-enforcement stings ever conducted in Las Vegas.

Miller was assigned to Switch in an administrative support role.

The Fencing Sting

The task force decided that the best way to catch the bad guys was to set up a stolen-property fencing business run by law enforcement. A storefront was rented on Western Avenue, an area consisting primarily of light-industrial businesses. The building was modified to include two-way mirrors for filming transactions and a fake wall that could be dropped to allow rapid access of additional forces into the business area if necessary.

Metro, the lead agency, provided two officers for the undercover portion of the operation. These officers actually ran the store and dealt directly with the crooks. The FBI handled the filming and audio recording of the illegal transactions. The DA's people provided support in the form of handling and cataloging evidence and preparing and maintaining related paperwork,

including warrant applications. These administrative support duties were mainly performed at a safe house about two miles from the Western Avenue location. In addition, the DA's investigators provided relief for the FBI agents doing the filming and recording at the storefront and would respond with shotguns if anyone attempted to rob the store.

Everything was in place when the storefront opened on June 15. Word was put out on the street that there was a new outlet where stolen property could be disposed of. The two Metro undercover men portrayed themselves as members of an organized-crime group from California. They acted the part and dressed accordingly. Jack Miller describes them as looking rather "seedy." One of the cops even wore an eye patch, but had to remove it when he developed a severe skin irritation.

The storefront had to be available to the lawbreakers from about mid-morning until late at night. That meant personnel needed to be assigned for more than 12 hours per day, seven days a week. It also meant a lot of overtime and a lot of boredom.

"The boredom was a big enemy to the crew at first," Miller recalled. "It would only take five or ten minutes for the illegal transaction. Then there would be about an hour for all of the administrative stuff. Money had to be accounted for, officer reports written, audio and videotapes reviewed and marked for evidence. Then it would be sit around and wait for the next customer. To combat the tedium a foosball table was purchased and several magazines were brought in daily. But after things got rolling, there was little time for such luxuries."

Business Boomed

As word of their fencing operation circulated, the cops soon found they had a booming business on their hands. They took in stolen merchandise ranging from credit cards—with related identification—to car radios, stereos, small office equipment, and guns. And while the visitors to the store— many of them repeats—"sold" their stolen loot, the cameras and recorders rolled.

Not all the items the police bought were small, however. Several hot cars were purchased and they once bought an 18-wheeler fully loaded with sugar.

"We didn't buy junk cars," Miller said. "Mercedes and Cadillac were common makes for us to take in." One such Caddy would eventually lead to Switch being shut down.

By necessity, Operation Switch was conducted in great secrecy.

Only those law-enforcement personnel with a need to know were let in on the scam. However, other police units were pursuing the same thieves as Switch.

One day, Jack Miller even bumped into a detective who turned out to be investigating the storefront!

"We're in an elevator going up to the DA's Office," Miller remembers. "We get talking and the guy tells me he's uncovered a big fencing operation on Western Avenue. He says he's on his way to see the DA and get a warrant to raid the place. As soon as we got off the elevator, I told my boss what was going on. The detective didn't get his warrant, but he was brought in on the sting."

As the months passed, the con was working beautifully. Stacks of recordings were piling up in the DA's Office and the inventory of recovered stolen property was impressive. And then the Caddy came into the picture.

A Bigger Crime

In November, three guys showed up at the store with a car they wanted to unload. It was a new Cadillac Seville, worth about $12,000, with Nevada plates on it. The men in possession of it were willing to let it go for $600.

The deal set off alarm bells in

the minds of the experienced undercover cops. They specifically asked the three thieves if there was any violence connected with the car. The suspects assured them it was simply a stolen car—nothing more than that. The deal was made and the cops took in the Caddy for the $600. During the transaction the suspects mentioned that they had pulled a drugstore robbery that was unrelated to the stolen vehicle.

A subsequent Department of Motor Vehicles check revealed that the car was registered to Lloyd Brooker, a sales manager at Cashman Cadillac. It turned out that Brooker was the subject of a missing-person report. He'd last been seen at a store buying an anniversary present for his wife. Now the alarm bells started clanging all over town.

A rush meeting was convened, including District Attorney George Holt and Sheriff Ralph Lamb, to discuss the situation. Although Brooker's body hadn't been found, it was almost a certainty he'd met with foul play and was probably dead. The case had to take priority over Switch; there was no doubt about it. But apprehending the possible killers prematurely based on their possession of the car would expose the sting, possibly endangering the undercover officers and giving crooks it had taken months to ensnare a chance to flee or hide.

To avoid those risks, it was imperative that Switch be quickly brought to a conclusion. The question was how.

One of the undercover cops mentioned that he had bantered with some burglars about how much his organization appreciated all the loot flowing in. He'd even said that at some point they'd throw an "appreciation party" to honor all the hard work the thieves had been doing.

"What if we throw the party now?" the cop wondered. "As they come in, we'll bust 'em."

After additional debate, the principals decided that the party idea provided the best chance for a successful and rapid conclusion to Switch. Word of the party would be put out on the street immediately. The thieves would be told that the store operators would provide "coke and broads" and would give away a Corvette. The cops didn't mention that the "coke" would be Coca-Cola and the "broads" drinking it would be female police officers.

To prevent the Brooker suspects from taking off in the meantime, they'd be detained on suspicion of the drugstore robbery.

While arrangements for the finale were being completed, a father and son doing some target shooting in the desert discovered the battered body of Lloyd Brooker. The pending charges against the 58 suspects caught up in Operation Switch now ranged from possession of stolen property to murder.

The Party

When the night of the gala arrived, one of the undercover officers told the guests that because their "big boss" was in attendance, it was necessary to frisk everyone before they could enter. He patted down the suspects in an anteroom, then passed them into the store area one at a time.

Once inside, the other cop said that he wanted to make sure the new arrival would be able to recognize his boss so that he could show proper respect. He asked the suspect to look at the back of the door he'd just passed through.

Hanging on the door was a picture of a smiling Sheriff Ralph Lamb. Every suspect was stunned and did a double or triple take as he tried to figure out what was going on. The last time his eyes returned to the officer, the cop flashed his badge and said: "I work for him. You're under arrest." At that point the fake wall opened and several uniformed officers emerged to take the suspect into custody.

Twenty-six of the alleged criminals were arrested that night. The rest were apprehended over the next several days. All 58 were subsequently convicted or entered guilty pleas to the charges originating from Switch. The killers of Lloyd Brooker were convicted of his murder.

Operation Switch was lauded as a tremendous success. Its organizers and all involved personnel were praised for their dedication and professionalism. It was also heralded as an example of what could be achieved through cooperative efforts between law-enforcement agencies. A speech paying tribute to Switch was made on the floor of the United States Senate.

However, success and professionalism are sometimes in the eye of the beholder. Not everyone was impressed with the conduct of Operation Switch.

One of the arrestees wrote a letter to the *Las Vegas Review-Journal* expressing a dissenting opinion. The paper printed the letter on December 14, 1976.

This individual felt that he'd been a victim of police trickery. He was an unemployed drug addict and the cops had taken advantage of his weaknesses, he argued. He thought it was particularly unfair that the lawmen had encouraged him to bring his dope with him to the party.

His final complaint may have rankled him the most: He never even got to see the car that was supposed to be given away to the best thief.

The Evolution Of SWAT

On July 4, 1976, the Tactical Unit changed its name to Special Weapons and Tactics. SWAT personnel were armed with fully automatic M-16s and M-76 9mm submachine guns. The unit was structured with two teams, Red and Blue, each consisting of a lieutenant, sergeant, and five officers.

Dwight Mahan was one of the sergeants assigned to SWAT at its inception and remained with the unit until transferring to Air Support in 1980. During a February 2003, interview he talked about the early days of SWAT.

"One of the problems at the start was that officers were assigned to SWAT on a part-time basis. Guys were scattered all around at different posts. When something came down, the team had to be rounded up before you could respond. It was even difficult to schedule training. You had to contact the sergeant the officer worked for and see if he'd let him attend the training; if his immediate supervisor couldn't spare him, that officer didn't get to attend the session."

Before Mahan left

for his new duty, SWAT had become a full-time assignment. When they weren't busy with hostage situations, barricaded gunmen, or executing search or arrest warrants regarding dangerous felons, officers trained, trained, and trained some more.

Lieutenant Larry Burns is the current SWAT Commander. In his 17 years with Metro, he's served with Patrol, Gangs, on the Police Academy staff, and in Criminal Intelligence. He assumed his present position in April 2002.

"We have a very highly trained and capable group of officers," Burns said of SWAT in December 2002. "Candidates applying for positions have to meet rigid physical requirements and be proficient

Special Weapons and Tactics (SWAT)—1976

with firearms. Our equipment is top-of-the-line, too."

That doesn't necessarily mean, however, that when SWAT is called to an incident, a violent end for the bad guy is inevitable.

"Our mission is to save lives, not take them. We have skilled negotiators who can communicate with suspects in a variety of languages. We can bring most situations to a peaceful conclusion using verbal skills. Because of the high level of training, we're much better able to resolve intense situations without injury to suspects or officers. There are occasions when deadly force is the only option, but those incidents are rare," Burns explained.

SWAT handles about 60 incidents per year in which a felony has been committed or an individual has been deemed to pose a danger to the community. All hostage situations and barricaded gunmen are SWAT territory. They also execute approximately 250 high-risk search warrants each year.

Since 1990, six SWAT officers have been shot in the line of duty. All survived and returned to work.

SWAT in field training

Spilotro, Part One

A name that became linked to scandal within Metro was Detective Joe Blasko. An officer with the LVPD prior to the merger, Blasko got into trouble for allegedly beating Jack Turner, a suspect whom Blasko arrested during a tumultuous strike by cab drivers in 1966. Turner died three days later and a coroner's inquest ruled the death was the result of excessive use of force by the arresting officers. Murder charges were filed against Blasko and his partner, Bruce Sandholm. They were later dismissed when a judge ruled there was insufficient evidence to prosecute.

Officer Blasko was back in the headlines in 1978. At that time, organized-crime figure Anthony Spilotro was residing in Las Vegas. It was believed he'd been sent to town by the Chicago mob to keep tabs on their casino interests. When he wasn't occupied with those duties, he kept busy doing loan sharking and running a crew of burglars called the "Hole in the Wall Gang." This nickname arose from the gang's penchant for entering the victim's business by cutting a hole in the back or side wall. Also known as "the Ant" (he was 5' 6"), Tony Spilotro was a suspect in some 20 murders nationwide. Naturally, he was the target of investigations by several agencies, including the FBI and Metro.

A man in Spilotro's line of work has special needs in order to stay in business. One of them is the ability to obtain information as to what the cops are up to, where bugs have been planted, and who might be tailing him. With ample resources, the Ant was able to find providers of that intelligence in Metro's own Organized-Crime Unit. His sources were Detective Joe Blasko and Sgt. Philip Leone.

An investigation of the two cops and their relationship with Spilotro and other mobsters resulted in indictments against the pair. Blasko was charged with racketeering and obstruction of justice. Sheriff Ralph Lamb fired him in June 1978. Leone, who had already retired for medical reasons, was charged with bribery. The cases against both men were later dropped.

The McCarthy Era

The Ralph Lamb Era Ends

Blasko and Leone weren't the only ones at Metro with legal troubles at the time. Ralph Lamb himself was fighting a 1977 indictment for income-tax evasion. The IRS alleged that Lamb spent more money than he earned. It was a charge that, if proved, meant Lamb had unreported income he hadn't paid taxes on. They further contended that he received "loans," including one for $30,000 from casino owner Benny Binion, that were never meant to be repaid and would therefore be taxable.

Although Sheriff Lamb was

acquitted of all charges in U.S. District Court, the trial and the events leading up to it occurred during the campaign season for the 1978 election. Politically wounded by the scandal and with his attention elsewhere, the 18-year incumbent, often referred to as "Mr. Metro," was defeated by his challenger, Metro's Vice and Narcotics Commander, John McCarthy.

McCarthy was born in Union City, New Jersey, on March 4, 1934. After being discharged from the Marine Corps in 1956, he came to Las Vegas and was hired by the LVPD that September. After consolidation, he rose to the rank of Commander in 1975. From there he challenged and beat his boss, Ralph Lamb. McCarthy ran as a "reform" candidate, promising to clean up Metro's Organized-Crime Unit after the devastating Spilotro scandal.

A former McCarthy associate described him as "a good cop, but naive politically." Others, both friend and foe, share that opinion. Even those who didn't support him say McCarthy had great integrity and character and wanted to do a good job. By all accounts, he was an honest man with good intentions. However, intentions aside, McCarthy's tenure was the most controversial and divisive in Metro's brief history.

It must be noted that while

John McCarthy

Sheriff McCarthy's own decisions may have caused some of the problems, others were inherited and still others were rumors that were never proved true. Allegations that McCarthy was the target of mob influence or was supported by the mob fall into the latter category. In fact, rather than being indifferent to the organized-crime problem, it was a top priority of his administration. The relationship and cooperation between the FBI and Metro actually flourished while McCarthy was in office. Their joint efforts marked the beginning of the end of the Spilotro era. Rumors to the contrary are included in the following paragraphs solely to give a more complete picture of the myriad problems with which Sheriff McCarthy had to contend while he was in office.

Troubles from the Start

Hopes were high for the new Sheriff, but before he was even sworn in he made a decision that alienated many Metro officers. Soon after the election, he announced that he intended to appoint several detectives and patrolmen to command positions, passing over personnel who had much more time and experience with Metro or its predecessors. This decision resulted in 39 officers filing a class-action lawsuit on December 28, 1978, challenging the legality of McCarthy's appointments. Although a court ruled in Sheriff McCarthy's favor in January 1979, the hard feelings would remain. In addition, he began his term by locking horns with the County Commissioners and City Councilmen over a variety of budgetary and policy issues. These skirmishes continued on and off for his entire term.

To honor his campaign promise, McCarthy appointed Detective Kent Clifford as Commander of the newly named Intelligence Bureau. Clifford's job was to restore integrity and confidence in this much-maligned section. Moving quickly, Clifford announced in January 1979 that his department had been reorganized, personnel moves had been made, and the Intelligence Bureau was "clean" to the best of his knowledge. That March, Metro was reinstated into the California Narcotics Intelligence Network, an organization from which it had been suspended for nine months due to information leaks involving the Spilotro investigation.

Clifford's declaration did not permanently end questions about his operation, however. As Sheriff McCarthy and his troops engaged in battle against the Spilotro gang, the Intelligence Bureau and its tactics remained a source of ongoing controversy.

While he was dealing with all these early problems, McCarthy had to defend himself and Metro from yet another assault: the attempt by Las Vegas City Councilmen to deconsolidate. Claiming that having their own police department would provide the city with better and cheaper police protection, the City

Kent Clifford

Council drafted a bill that would split Metro. And, as if McCarthy needed any more fuel on the fire, a simultaneous report surfaced claiming that organized-crime was attempting to gain influence over him and mob money had paid for his post-election victory party. These were charges that he vehemently denied and were never proven.

As 1979 wore on, yet more troubling issues surfaced. In September, it was revealed that McCarthy had filled the newly created position of Fiscal Analyst with a convicted felon. The man actually was still in prison, serving a four-year prison sentence for embezzlement. Starting October 1, he would begin performing his duties for Metro on a work-release program until his sentence was completed. The Sheriff defended his selection, pointing out that the man had made complete restitution, came highly recommended, and would not be involved with the collection or distribution of Metro funds. That same month, McCarthy filed to divorce his wife of 22 years.

Racial Misconduct

In October, Metro was accused of mistreating blacks and harassing two businessmen who had complained about questionable police tactics. In the first instance, the local chapter of the NAACP charged that some police officers operated under the premise that all blacks were criminals, or at least prone to crime, and weren't entitled to the rights afforded other citizens. McCarthy admitted that misconduct sometimes occurred in a department with 900 sworn personnel. He said, however, that any "abuse" against blacks involved disrespect, rather than physical mistreatment. He added that an investigation of one officer for possible misconduct had already begun and others were pending. He also said that he wanted to establish a dialogue with the black community to make sure similar complaints were handled justly.

The second case involved two gun-shop owners who'd been arrested for criminal possession of brass knuckles, a gross misdemeanor. After being charged, both men questioned the tactics employed by the Intelligence Division during the investigation that led to their arrests. The pair claimed that after making their complaint, they received anonymous threatening phone calls, which they believed were from the police. They alleged that a female police informant they knew told them the cops were planning to retaliate against them. Sheriff McCarthy promised to lunch an Internal Affairs investigation and expressed confidence in the department's ability to investigate itself.

Politics, Enemies List, and Organized Crime

The year ended with continuing controversy over the issue of building a new jail, a matter that dogged Sheriff McCarthy for the next three years.

January 1980 began with the news that the homicide rate in Clark County had reached a record high and the overall crime rate was also on the rise. At the start of February, McCarthy's son was arrested for selling narcotics to an undercover officer. The investigation was conducted with the Sheriff's knowledge and to his credit, he made no effort to influence how the case was handled.

Shortly after that, District Judge Joseph Pavlikowski ruled the law that had created the Metropolitan Police Department was unconstitutional, awarding the proponents of deconsolidation a major victory. Sheriff McCarthy declared the decision "a severe blow to the concept of Metro" and vowed to appeal the ruling. Judge Pavlikowski stayed the dissolution of Metro until the Sheriff's appeal could be heard by the Nevada Supreme Court. In addition to seeking relief in the courts, McCarthy appealed to the public to fight the attempt to split the agency. While the efforts of the City Councilmen to void the merger eventually failed, Sheriff McCarthy himself later became their target.

A bombshell appeared in the *Las Vegas Sun* on April 3, 1980. Two veteran lawmen believed they were under surveillance and investigation by Metro. One of the alleged victims was Beecher Avants, a former Metro detective who had resigned when McCarthy was elected. Avants was currently working as the Chief Investigator in the Clark County District Attorney's Office. The second man was John Moran, McCarthy's own Undersheriff. The Sheriff, who supposedly sanctioned the investigations, refused immediate comment. The article did point out, however, that both Moran and Avants were potential candidates to oppose McCarthy in the 1982 election.

The *Review-Journal* ran a parallel story the same day. It reported that Metro, under Sheriff McCarthy's direction, was compiling an "enemies list" consisting of political opponents, reporters, and other prominent Las Vegans. County Commissioner Manny Cortez said he heard from Metro insiders that he'd been under investigation for six months and that "compromising" information had been developed.

In a press conference the following day, Sheriff McCarthy denied the allegations. He said the stories were an attempt to discredit the Intelligence Bureau and Commander Kent Clifford. Mc-

Carthy further announced that he intended to take some unspecified disciplinary action against Moran for making comments to the media. Four days later John Moran was fired, but he vowed to fight his dismissal.

The *Las Vegas Sun* reported on June 5 that Moran had won a decision in his contested firing. Judge Pavlikowski ordered that the former Undersheriff be reinstated with all back pay and benefits on June 17. John Moran returned to his job on the designated date and announced his resignation just over a week later. Stating that he and McCarthy "will never get together on anything," Moran said he'd leave his position on July 11.

Also on June 5, a page-two headline in *The Valley Times* read: "Metro Police Battle Erupts At City Hall." The story cited a resolution calling for the city to keep the "concept" of Metro. The document was reportedly developed in a meeting between Mayor Bill Briare, Sheriff McCarthy, and County Commission Chairman Sam Bowler. The city representatives were enraged, stating the resolution was the equivalent of dropping their lawsuit to dissolve Metro. They were also angry over not having been included in the meeting that had generated the document.

At approximately 11:45 p.m. on Monday June 9, two undercover Metro Intelligence officers shot and killed a suspect they'd been following. The dead man, Frank Daniel Bluestein, age 35, was a maitre d' at the Hacienda Hotel. Also known as Frankie Blue, he reportedly had ties to organized-crime figures, including Tony Spilotro.

In a series of stories beginning the following day, the *Review-Journal* reported that a Metro spokesman had confirmed that Bluestein had been under surveillance for several hours prior to the shooting. The police version of events was that the victim met with Tony Spilotro, the original subject of the surveillance, at a restaurant earlier in the evening. At that time, the officers didn't know Bluestein's identity. When the meeting broke up, the cops decided to follow Bluestein to learn who he was and what he was up to. After tailing him for a while, Bluestein allegedly committed an unspecified traffic violation. With that infraction providing probable cause, the officers stopped the vehicle. With the flashing red light activated on the dash of their unmarked car, the cops followed Bluestein for several blocks, then parked their car at a right angle to Bluestein's and exited their vehicle, identifying themselves as police officers. Bluestein started to get out of the Lincoln, allegedly brandishing a .22 handgun. Believing the suspect intended to shoot at them, the officers fired ten rounds, some of which struck Bluestein in the chest and stomach. He died at Sunrise Hospital a short time later.

Not satisfied with the police explanation, Bluestein's family hired criminal-defense attorney, and future Mayor of Las Vegas, Oscar Goodman to look into the matter. Goodman already counted Tony Spilotro among his clients. A coroner's inquest ruled Bluestein's death a case of justifiable homicide. A $22 million lawsuit filed against Metro and the two detectives by Oscar Goodman on behalf of the Bluestein family was later adjudicated in favor of the police. While these issues were being settled, they continued to get substantial news coverage and resulted in steady sniping between Goodman and Sheriff McCarthy.

In April 1981, a special three-member Senate panel conducted a hearing in Carson City in regard to the continuing battle between Las Vegas and Clark County over Metro. The panel subsequently made recommendations that were incorporated into Senate Bill 386, a measure intended to "clean up" the 1973 act that had created Metro and had later been ruled unconstitutional. In often heated debate, the city officials proposed that a Chief of Police be appointed to run the department commencing in January 1983. This would relegate the role of the Sheriff to minor duties, such as serving civil papers and running the county jail. This plan was strongly opposed by Sheriff Mc Carthy and Clark County. McCarthy argued that the voters should select the chief law-enforcement officer in Clark County.

A few weeks later, the same representatives who'd been at each other's throats for months met again in Carson City. This time the mood was much different as they were gathered to announce that an agreement had been reached over Metro. The City of Las Vegas and Clark County concurred that SB386 was constitutional and that the police department should be funded in a fair manner. Under the new financial arrangements, Clark County paid 54.9% of Metro's cost, up from its previous 53% share. This represented about a $4 million increase for Clark County taxpayers and an equal windfall for Las Vegas residents. Although the city did quite well financially, Las Vegas officials did make a major political concession by dropping their request that a Chief of Police be appointed to run Metro; Sheriff McCarthy would remain in charge. The deconsolidation battle was over and it would be many years before the issue was raised again.

Sheriff McCarthy had little time to celebrate his victory before learning that John Moran was organizing a campaign to unseat him in the next election. The former Undersheriff told a *Las Vegas Sun* reporter that even though he hadn't officially declared his candidacy, he had a lot of workers passing the word that he intended to be in the race.

Another issue surfaced in 1981 that caused Sheriff McCarthy additional headaches. Though the world's oldest profession, prostitution, was illegal in Clark County, *The Valley Times* ran a story on November 3 stating that tourists couldn't walk outside the resorts without being accosted by a working girl. The piece cited a statistic

---

Two Officers Down

James Walter Harbin

While on his way to work on March 18, 1979, Corrections Officer James Walter Harbin II decided to stop at a convenience store for an unknown item. Dressed in a uniform almost identical to that worn by the street cops, he walked into a robbery in progress. The suspect, thinking that Harbin was a police officer responding to the robbery, shot the twenty-two-year-old as he entered the store. The killer was subsequently apprehended. His parents survived Officer Harbin.

On August 12, 1979, Officer Clark Anthony Wooldridge was responding to a fight and accident call. On the way, his patrol car collided with another vehicle and overturned. The 22-year-old was pinned under his car. He was extricated, but died at the hospital. The call to which he was traveling turned out to be a false alarm; there was no fight or accident. Officer Wooldridge's wife of less than two years survived him.

Clark Anthony Wooldridge

that 15,000 prostitution-related arrests had been made so far that year, with a scant 48 convictions. McCarthy responded that he didn't have the staff and money to institute the necessary foot patrols to effectively deal with the problem and that the laws were insufficient. The District Attorney said he couldn't do much with bad arrests and weak cases. The judges said they could only impose sentences based on the laws currently on the books. Whatever the reasons, more aggressive enforcement was demanded and that responsibility rested with Sheriff McCarthy.

To close out the year, McCarthy's son—already on probation for a drug conviction—was arrested for driving under the influence of alcohol or drugs following a traffic accident on Flamingo Road.

McCarthy Fights for His Job

Compared to the previous years, 1982 began calmly for Sheriff McCarthy and Metro, or so it appeared on the surface. Behind the scenes, however, much political activity was taking place. Several candidates had announced their intentions to oppose the Sheriff in the upcoming November election. In fact, John McCarthy was being challenged from within his own party and would have to win in a primary even to make it to the general election. He was the incumbent and was favored to be the nominee, but in politics, nothing can be taken for granted. If he won the primary, he'd likely be facing his former second-in-command, John Moran, in the main event.

Moran officially announced his candidacy in early April; later that month things began to heat up. Old allegations resurfaced and found their way into the press. McCarthy's supposed "political enemies list" received a lot of ink, with an equal number of denials by the sheriff. The rumors that McCarthy had been corrupted by mob money made an encore appearance. The sheriff again vehemently refuted the charges, dismissing them as part of a smear campaign by his opponents.

In June, another scandal broke. A former Metro detective was arrested by Intelligence Bureau officers and charged with operating a burglary ring that preyed on drug dealers. The burglars supposedly identified drug dealers, then broke into their homes, taking money, jewelry, and drugs. Although the suspect, Larry Gandy, reportedly told detectives that no other current or former Metro officers were involved, several cops were expected to submit to polygraph examinations.

When interviewed by reporters from the *Las Vegas Sun*, Gandy leveled another charge against the Intelligence Bureau's boss, Kent Clifford. He claimed that Clifford had once directed him to rough up a criminal suspect. Gandy said he complied with the order by breaking the suspect's nose.

The Intelligence Bureau and Sheriff McCarthy took another hit almost simultaneously, when a Metro detective accused Clifford of allowing a confidential informant to sell cocaine on the street three years earlier. According to the allegation, the informant had purchased three ounces of cocaine from a casino executive. He turned the information and drugs over to Clifford and wanted to be reimbursed. Clifford didn't want to pay $2,500 for evidence in what he thought was a weak case, but he didn't want to lose a valuable informant either. As a compromise, he told the informant to sell the drugs in order to get his money back. These charges, too, were denied and attributed to dirty politics. The media questioned John Moran about the drug allegations against Clifford. He denied having any role in the release of the information.

In late July, the District Attorney's Office announced that there was insufficient evidence to charge Kent Clifford with any wrongdoing in the cocaine case. Metro officers opposed to Sheriff McCarthy complained the investigation was

a whitewash. McCarthy and Clifford maintained the whole episode was unfounded and politically motivated.

After McCarthy and Moran won their respective primaries in September, things got really nasty, with Tony Spilotro's money becoming an issue yet again.

It started later that month when a mobster who'd turned government informant claimed that Spilotro not only had donated $40,000 to Moran's campaign, but also supplied liquor for campaign parties. The informant, Frank Cullotta, said Spilotro's largesse was given in return for a promise that Moran, if elected, would leave the mobster alone. Moran emphatically denied the allegations, blaming the McCarthy people for perpetrating the "out-and-out lies." The challenger followed up two days later by announcing he had taken a lie-detector test that proved Cullotta's story was baseless.

Sheriff McCarthy admitted he had heard about the accusations, but said he had absolutely nothing to do with their becoming public.

In early October, Moran came under more fire for dropping out of a televised debate with McCarthy on KLAS-TV. Moran refused to appear, stating that one of the panelists was a staunch McCarthy supporter and biased in his reporting.

A week later, a story surfaced

in the *Las Vegas Sun* that Sheriff McCarthy had received a $2,000 contribution from Joe Conforte, a fugitive Nevada brothel owner, during his 1978 campaign against Ralph Lamb. McCarthy admitted receiving the money, but said it was through a third party and the name of the actual donor had been unknown to him. After that initial admission, the details became somewhat fuzzy, however. Undersheriff Don Denison, who kept the campaign's books, said the $2,000 was paid by cashier's check. Chuck Thompson, the "third party" who actually handed over the contribution, disagreed. "No, it was not a cashier's check. It was $2,000 cash," he is reported as saying. There was no record of a donation in that amount from either Thompson or Conforte on file with the Secretary of State.

On October 20, McCarthy attacked Moran's character in a *Review-Journal* article. He accused his challenger of conducting a campaign based on slanted commercials and fraudulent statements to the press. McCarthy further claimed that these falsehoods weren't an accident; Moran was knowingly lying. "I wonder what else he's lying about to deceive the people of Clark County," McCarthy said.

Moran launched a counterattack, challenging McCarthy and Kent Clifford to submit to polygraph exams to prove they hadn't been responsible for spreading the story about Moran receiving money from Spilotro. Both McCarthy and Clifford declined Moran's invitation, stating the issue was a matter between Moran and Frank Cullotta.

As October ended, Moran was winning endorsement after endorsement, while polls showed that the incumbent was pulling only 29% of the vote. Time was running short for Sheriff McCarthy.

Moran Wins

On November 2, John Moran won a resounding victory. During his campaign, Moran had pledged to clean up the prostitution problem, crack down on schoolyard drug pushers, declare war on teenage gangs, and use Civil Service rules rather than politics to appoint Metro officials. Starting in two months, the voters would see what their selection had gotten them.

In addition to politics and scandal, other notable events that occurred while John McCarthy was in office included the deaths of two more Metro officers, an inmate takeover of the jail, a fatal fire at the MGM Grand Hotel and Casino, and the establishment of a new unit to handle the ever-increasing volume of special events coming to Las Vegas.

Takeover!

At approximately nine o'clock on the morning of August 25, 1979, inmates took control of the Jail Annex, located on the second floor of the Las Vegas City Hall complex on Stewart Avenue. This was the longest siege ever handled by the Las Vegas Metropolitan Police Department. The incident had all the ingredients of a Hollywood action movie: hardcore cons facing long sentences with little to lose, security equipment not working, procedures not followed, and escape within the grasp of the inmates, though they didn't know it. Future Sheriff Jerry Keller, a sergeant at the time, was the primary negotiator for the police side.

McKenna, Lorenzo, and Shaw

That Saturday morning began routinely. At that time, the Annex was used primarily to house sentenced prisoners—mostly felons awaiting transfer to the state prison system in Carson City. On this particular day, 84 inmates were housed in the Annex.

Among them were Patrick McKenna, Felix Lorenzo, and Eugene Shaw. McKenna and Lorenzo had recently been transferred to the Annex after having been implicated in a plot to start a riot at the Clark County Detention Center.

McKenna was a 33-year-old white male with a long history of problems with the law. An escape artist and convicted rapist, he was serving three life sentences plus 75 years for sexually assaulting two women in Las Vegas in 1978. He was also facing a murder charge for killing his cellmate while housed in the Clark County Detention Center.

Lorenzo, a Latino, was 30 years old at the time. He'd been sentenced to 160 years in prison for numerous armed robberies. He'd taken hostages during his capers, on one occasion briefly holding captive an off-duty Metro officer. He was no stranger to prison strife, having been incarcerated at the Attica Correctional Facility in New York State during the infamous riot in 1971.

Shaw, a 41-year-old black male, was another convicted armed robber, doing a 60-year sentence.

What these convicts did that morning was not a spur-of-the-moment act. On the contrary, it was a well-planned escape attempt devised after a careful study of guard activities and jail procedures. The plot included paying an inmate trustee to leave ajar a security gate that led to the gun lockers where correction officers stored their service weapons. The warning light that would have alerted the guard in the Control Booth of the open door had been out of service for some time due to a mechanical malfunction. Whether this was known by the prisoners or a matter of pure luck is unclear.

In addition to these three prisoners, three correction officers were to play major roles in the incident as hostages. David Murray, age 35, Robert Hansen, 52, and William Melton, also 52, were all veteran officers with many years of experience.

The Inmates Take Control

At a few minutes after nine that morning, Eugene Shaw completed mopping the floor of the cellblock in which he, Lorenzo, and McKenna were housed. Officer Hansen was observing Shaw through the glass panel of the cellblock's locked security door. The officer later said that he'd never seen any of the inmates in that particular block work so hard.

Another door allowing access to the hallway outside the cellblock door was unlocked and open. Although contrary to policy and procedure, this door was apparently routinely left unsecured.

Inmate Shaw advised Hansen that he had finished his work and the cleaning materials could be removed from the cellblock. He pushed the nearly full mop pail toward the security door.

Hansen opened the door without first locking the inmates in their cells. He then bent over to grab the heavy bucket and lift it over the raised threshold. As he did, Shaw said, "Here, that's heavy; let me give you a hand."

Using this ruse, Shaw approached the stooped-over guard and struck him on the back of the neck. Before he fell, Hansen was able to reach up and activate an alarm button in a control panel next to the door.

Inmate Lorenzo, who had been in the cell-block's day room, joined Shaw and finished overpowering Hansen—beating the officer until he was nearly unconscious. Correction Officer Murray, responding to the alarm, was also taken hostage.

Lorenzo removed the key to the gun locker from Hansen's pocket and exited the cellblock. Crouching low to avoid detection by the security cameras, he arrived at the gun-locker gate, which the trustee accomplice had left open. In a few seconds, he had possession of Hansen's 9mm semi-automatic pistol. After arming himself, Lorenzo located the remaining guard, William Melton, in the booking area and took him prisoner at gunpoint. The Annex was now entirely in the control of the criminals.

Joined by McKenna, the three inmates stripped the guards, donned their uniforms and were ready for their escape. Unfortunately for them, they didn't realize that the elevator located next to the gun lockers and controlled from the main Control Booth would have taken them to the first floor and freedom. Instead, they attempted to exit the front jail entrance, but were blocked by detectives who had responded to the alarm activated by Officer Hansen. The inmates retreated back into the interior of the jail, where the captured guards had been left handcuffed. The escape attempt was aborted and the incident turned into a hostage situation.

After letting a few selected inmates whom they trusted out of their cells, the three ringleaders returned to the gun lockers. They retrieved the service weapons of Officers Murray and Melton, along with a .380 semi-automatic pistol. This gave the bad guys an arsenal of four handguns, three loaded 9mm magazines, and a box of ammunition for the .380.

As they searched through the facility, they came across something almost as valuable to them as the weapons: a complete department Policy and Procedure Manual.

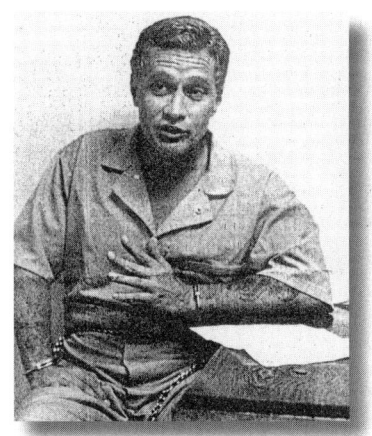
Patrick McKenna

While watching for police activity on the TV monitors covering the entrances, the convicts could now read about how the cops planned to respond to various jail incidents, how SWAT units would be deployed, and the techniques that might be used by Metro negotiators.

The Cops Respond

Outside the jail, uniformed personnel quickly contained the exterior of the building; two six-man SWAT teams were put into position in the corridor outside the jail entrance and elsewhere in the immediate area.

The recently created Hostage Negotiation Team made contact with the inmates via the cellblock phone system. Felix Lorenzo identified himself as the spokesman for the convicts; Patrick McKenna was later identified as the "security chief." For the next several hours, Lorenzo refused to discuss a resolution to the standoff directly with the police. Instead, he insisted on face-to-face meetings with specific local newsmen and attorneys whom he felt could be trusted more than the lawmen. The situation remained deadlocked until the police agreed to arrange for the requested third-party mediators.

Each side had concerns about the other that needed to be resolved before meetings could begin. The cops were afraid that the mediator could be a tempting target for the inmates to add to their cache of hostages. The inmates worried about a forced entry by a SWAT team and that their negotiator might get picked off or captured during the negotiating sessions.

To discourage a police assault, the felons periodically moved their hostages around, handcuffing them in close proximity to various points of entry.

The safety of the negotiators was addressed in a mutual agreement. A table was placed half in and half out of the jail-entrance door. This allowed the inmate negotiator—either Lorenzo or McKenna—to sit at the enclosed end of the table with limited exposure. The civilian mediator would remain in the open and be less apt to be harmed or taken prisoner by the convicts.

For further protection of the mediator, the police assigned a marksman to a position in a nearby parking structure whenever meetings were in progress. Overlooking the negotiating table at a distance of about 25 yards, the sniper was under instructions to shoot if it appeared the third party was in danger of being harmed or taken prisoner. As an additional precaution, several SWAT members were concealed in a stairwell close to the meeting site, ready to respond quickly to any threatening behavior by the inmates.

A member of the Hostage Negotiation Team, too, was out of sight, but within earshot of the sessions.

Inmate Demands

Eighteen hours after the initial takeover, a list consisting of 10 inmate demands was presented to Deputy Public Defender Tom Leen, one of the mediators approved by the convicts. They related to such things as the availability of a law library and medical services and improved visitation, phone calls, and food.

Most of these concerns had previously been brought to the attention of jail authorities through the appropriate channels and found to have some merit. Changes were in fact being developed at the time of the takeover.

While the police were preparing responses to the initial demands, they maintained phone contact with Lorenzo and McKenna. Just prior to noon on Sunday, McKenna asked for newspapers, inmate mail, and medication.

After deliberation, the Metro negotiators decided to see what effect declining the requests would have. The refusal was delivered, along with an explanation for the decision. McKenna accepted the police position and those matters were dropped.

While these telephone conversations were going on, a relationship was developing between McKenna and police negotiator Sgt. Jerry Keller, a relationship that it was hoped would lead to the safe release of the hostage. Another mediator came on board, too. He was Bob Stoldal, News Director of KLAS-TV.

Bob Stoldal Mediates

Nearly 23 years later, Bob Stoldal still has vivid memories of his participation in the jail incident. He remembers that he was recruited as a mediator directly by Patrick McKenna.

"I was at the TV station when the phone rang; it was Patrick. He identified himself and the situation. I'd never met him before, but I knew his father. He said he knew who I was and that he wanted a member of the media to act as an intermediary between the inmates and the police. We discussed the issue and I agreed to come down to the jail, which I did," the reporter says.

Stoldal had a good relationship with Metro, having covered the cop beat for several years. They knew him personally, and his mother had worked in the records section of the Las Vegas Police Department.

"The table where I met with the inmates was positioned so that they would be sitting inside the room and couldn't get to me very easily. I stayed outside the room, leaving them about ten or twelve feet away from me and behind a high counter. That arrangement gave both of us some protection," Stoldal recalls.

"I would take food up to the inmates and bring messages back to the officers, more of a messenger than a negotiator," he continued. "I remember the first time I went up there alone to meet McKenna. I kept looking at him and asked if he was pointing a gun at me; he said he wasn't. Since I didn't see any upside to him shooting me, I tended to believe him. I don't know how many trips I made up those

Special Events Section

By this time, the late '70s and early '80s, Las Vegas was rapidly becoming a popular location for television and motion-picture filming, parades, sporting events, concerts, boxing matches, and the like. All of these activities required police coordination and participation.

In 1982, a Special Events Section was established to help plan and schedule officers to staff the 30 to 35 events per year. Lt. Dwight Mahan was assigned as coordinator of the new unit.

"We handled everything from major boxing matches to high-school sporting events, from marches and parades to concerts and movie shoots," Mahan recalled in February 2003.

"In addition to that, Special Events coordinated security for visiting dignitaries. If it was the president or vice president, we worked with the Secret Service. A head-of-state had Secret Service protection, too. If the visitor was below head-of-state, our State Department sent a security detail. We worked well together and never lost one of our guests."

In 2002, the Special Events Section handled 136 filmings/productions, 226 sporting events, 148 concerts, and 1,337 miscellaneous events, with a total of 91,359 man-hours worked.

---

stairs, but I'll tell you that the walk up always seemed longer than the walk back."

At one point, Metro wanted the inmates to show the newsman the hostages to verify their condition. "An image sticks in my mind of one of the guards being brought out behind the counter. I asked him how he was and he said he was okay. I remember he looked very scared and a little beat up," Stoldal says.

"I don't know as saying I felt threatened or afraid would be the right words," he explained. "You kind of get in a zone during something like that. I do remember that I always looked directly at the inmates so as not to show any fear and be as calm as possible, as conversational as possible. About the middle of the second day, one of the members of the negotiating team pulled me aside and kind of shook me. 'You've got to be more careful,' he warned me. He was concerned that I might be getting too friendly with the inmates. He wanted to remind me that these were the 'bad guys' and not to trust them. 'It's a matter of life or death,' he said."

Stoldal was aware of the sniper positioned in the parking garage and that he would be in the direct line of fire should the inmate make a move on him. He was under orders that if he felt threatened, he was to dive to his right behind a large metal trash container and crawl away. Thankfully, that never became necessary.

Years later, Stoldal joked with Jerry Keller, "Which way was I supposed to dive? I never could remember."

Violence Inside

As these meetings continued and the police pressed for the release of the captured guards, unbeknownst to Stoldal or the cops, things were deteriorating inside the jail. Although the inmates had allowed each of the hostages to telephone his family—viewed as a positive development—two of the ringleaders were in sharp disagreement over what to do next.

Felix Lorenzo reportedly wanted to kill Officer Murray over a previous altercation. Eugene Shaw

was allegedly concerned about what Lorenzo and McKenna might do and wanted to contain them so that he could surrender to the police.

At approximately 5:30 Monday morning, nearly 48 hours into the escape attempt, Sgt. Keller was on the phone with McKenna. The inmate was seated on the floor outside the door to the sergeant's office. Officer Melton was handcuffed to a chair nearby. In a major breakthrough, Keller convinced McKenna to release Melton as a sign of good faith.

Just as Keller was cradling the handset, he heard the sound of gunshots over the phone and im-

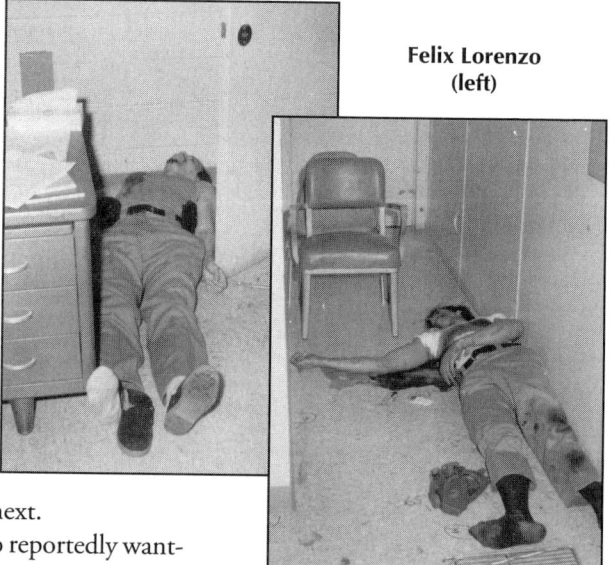

Felix Lorenzo (left)

Eugene Shaw

mediately called back. An inmate named Kuzman answered the phone. He advised Sgt. Keller that there had been a gunfight and that Shaw and Lorenzo were dead.

Kuzman was ordered to unload all weapons and surrender, an order with which he complied. McKenna stripped off the correction officer's uniform he was wearing and walked out of the jail with Officers Hansen and Murray to surrender. Officer Melton, who had sustained a minor hand wound during the shootout, remained inside. SWAT personnel cleared the facility and all of the inmates were subsequently transferred to the Clark County Detention Center.

In the investigation that followed, physical evidence and interviews with personnel and inmates were used to reconstruct the final moments of the siege.

It was determined that while McKenna was negotiating by phone with Sgt. Keller, Shaw and Lorenzo became engaged in a violent argument in a corridor a few feet from McKenna's location. Shooting erupted between the two, switching from position to position during the gunfight. Eventually, Lorenzo fell dead inside the sergeant's office, but not before wounding Shaw. During the gunfire, Officer Melton suffered a bullet wound to his left hand.

With Lorenzo disposed of,

Shaw turned his attention to McKenna, who was still inside the sergeant's office. The inmates swapped bullets; McKenna's aim was more accurate. Within a few seconds, Shaw joined Lorenzo as an ex-inmate.

McKenna Tries Again

Patrick McKenna was charged in Shaw's death, but was acquitted. He did, however, receive an additional 92-year sentence for his role in the takeover. In 1980 he was convicted of murdering his cellmate while in the Clark County Detention Center and was sentenced to death. In spite of this, his exploits were not over.

On February 14, 1981, McKenna attempted an escape from Nevada State Prison. At 7:35 that night, as he was being escorted to the showers, he produced a loaded handgun and took several correction officers and a nurse captive. He locked them up and attempted to find a way out of the building. The hostages were able to free themselves and escape. The condemned housing unit was soon surrounded and McKenna surrendered.

In January 1997, McKenna was among a group of death-row inmates who attempted an escape from the maximum-security prison in Ely. This effort was also thwarted.

During a death-house interview with KLAS-TV investigative reporter George Knapp that aired on May 20, 2002, McKenna spoke about that escape attempt: "I'm convinced in my head I beat this place," he said. "These guys might not agree, but in my head, I beat this place."

As the condemned man's various appeals grind on, it is too early to tell whether McKenna or the death chamber will claim the final victory.

Rescue!

At 7:20 a.m. on November 21,1980, police responded to assist the fire department at a major blaze at the MGM Grand Hotel (now Bally's) on the Strip. Traffic Division and K-9 personnel handled traffic and crowd control while other officers entered the burning building to conduct a room-to-room search for victims and survivors.

At approximately the same time, a Metro helicopter, manned by Sgt. Harry Christopher and Officer Tom Mildren, had just cleared from participating in a narcotics raid. Hearing the radio calls, they responded to the scene. They observed a large number of people on the roof of the 26-story building, where they had fled from the smoke and flames pursuing them; the size of the crowd was increasing steadily. As the people realized they were trapped, they became frantic.

Sergeant Christopher informed ground units of the situation, then landed the chopper on the roof. Officer Mildren exited the aircraft to stem the rush of the panic-stricken mob as they sought to get aboard their only means of escape. After making a radio request for assistance from additional helicopters, Sgt. Christopher left

Metro Helicopter

Officer Mildren on the roof and began a series of trips evacuating the crowd to the hotel's parking lot, where they were tended to by ground personnel. After the roof was cleared, Christopher and Mildren flew around the building searching for people trapped on balconies outside their upper-story rooms. They reported the locations of the victims to the search teams inside the hotel, then used their loudspeaker to provide assurances that help was on the way.

Eighty-five unfortunate souls perished in this disaster. Subsequent investigation determined that the incident started as a small electrical fire in one of the kitchens on the ground floor. Had the hotel been fully outfitted with automatic sprinklers, it was estimated the only harm done would have been water damage to the building.

The Moran Era

John Moran had barley occupied the Sheriff's office in January 1983 when he made a move to combat a relatively new gang of criminals: the Marielitos. These were Cubans who had come to the United States as part of the Marielito Boat Lift of 1980. The gang had concentrated in an area known as Tam Drive. Their crimes were becoming more and more frequent and violent, resulting in the establishment of the Tam Drive Foot Patrol. The goal of the officers assigned to this detail was to remove the Marielitos already in Las Vegas back to Cuba or prison and send a message to others contemplating coming to Vegas. The message would be clear: If you come here, you'll be dealt with swiftly and summarily.

Through 1984, the Foot Pa-

John Moran

trol was responsible for sending 90 Marielitos to either state or federal prison. The program was so effective it was cited in *Parade* magazine and was used as a guide by other cities to combat similar crime problems.

Working Girls

Another major issue for Sheriff Moran was to honor a campaign pledge to get rid of the prostitutes infesting the downtown and Strip areas within 90 days. Deputy Chief Steve Waugh of the Field Services Division was assigned the task of developing a plan that would make Moran's promise a reality. During a March 2003 interview, Steve Waugh explained what he did to carry out his orders.

"The prostitutes had become increasingly aggressive in their solicitation efforts," Waugh recalls. "They would often proposition men who were walking down the street with their wives, and invite the wives along to the party, too. Some of them weren't very gracious when they got turned down."

In January 1983 Waugh came up with a three-stage strategy, officially known as the Prostitution Suppression Program. Under his plan, the first 30 days would be used to gather intelligence and identify the prostitutes and their pimps. During the following month, the police would use that information to undertake intensive arrest and enforcement actions. The final phase concentrated on maintenance and making sure the gains made during the first 60 days stayed in place.

"Getting the prostitutes under control was a top priority of the department and the community. We had commitments from the District Attorney and the judges that they would support what we were doing. That backing was instrumental in making the program a success," Waugh says. "We also got a lot of press coverage, which helped to get the word out that we meant business."

Waugh drew on the Street Crime Attack Team, Vice, SWAT, and Uniformed Division for manpower. The SCAT and SWAT teams each supplied about 20 officers for plainclothes operations. Vice detectives had some involvement with the prostitutes, but concentrated primarily on the pimps. In addition to the personnel assigned directly to the endeavor, the entire department was told that combating the problem was everyone's responsibility. If a burglary detective was returning to the station and saw a hooker soliciting on Fremont Street, he or she was expected to take action. This approach added hundreds of additional officers to the effort.

After the prostitutes were arrested, they were transported to a facility called the Inmate Rehabilitation Farm, where they were processed, issued appearance tickets, and released. The farm was located several miles from the Strip and return transportation was not included in Metro's service. Pay phones were scarce and cell phones weren't standard equipment for prostitutes in those days. The arrestees, many in high heels, had to walk miles before they could call for a ride. The message was getting out.

Chief Waugh's plan worked to perfection: The great majority of prostitutes found new venues in which to ply their trade within the 90-day time frame. "Not only could we see the results ourselves, the success was confirmed when the police in Los Angeles, San Diego, and Phoenix started noticing our former prostitutes on their streets. They called us and wanted to know how we did it, so they could try it too," Waugh laughed.

Imitation may indeed be the most sincere form of flattery.

person engaging in criminal activity or endangering the public safety.

The strike began on April 2 and the situation quickly turned ugly. On April 3, a demonstrator attempted to stop the car of a temporary security guard from entering Caesars Palace. The striking Caesars' waiter threw himself across the hood of the guard's car, fell off, and ended up under the vehicle's wheels. He was hospitalized, but recovered.

Another picketer was hit by a car at the MGM the next day. This time the victim struck the vehicle of a non-striking worker with her picket sign as the driver attempted to cross the strike line. The driver put the car in reverse and ran the woman down. The police, who

Strike

On April 1, 1984, the Metropolitan Police Department was gearing up for a most unpleasant possibility: a major labor strike. Members of Culinary Local 226, the Bartender Union, Musicians Local 369, and Stagehands Local 720 were scheduled to walk off the job at midnight.

Sheriff Moran issued a statement saying Metro would remain neutral should a strike occur, but would arrest any

Metro arrests striker—1984

witnessed the incident, arrested the driver and charged him with battery with a deadly weapon. The victim suffered only minor injuries.

On April 14, the striking unions filed a $69 million civil-rights suit in U.S. District Court against the Nevada Resort Association hotels, their security guards, and Metro. The suit alleged that the defendants were denying union members the right to assemble, petition the government, be free from unreasonable searches and seizures, and receive equal protection under the law. When giving a statement to the press about the filing, the heads of the Stagehands and Musicians locals said the hotel security guards were acting like labor goons in the 1920s. Meanwhile, the union heads denied any knowledge of who had planted a bomb that detonated in the MGM swimming pool two nights earlier, saying that labor unions didn't engage in that type of activity.

Arrests and violence escalated as the strike continued. "I was a sergeant at the time, in charge of a squad at the intersection of Flamingo and the Strip. We arrested about a hundred people a night for the first two or three weeks," Assistant Sheriff Mike Zagorski said in a January 2003 interview.

Zagorski's troops numbered 19, seven or eight of whom were rookies. They worked from 3 p.m. until 3 a.m. daily for nearly two months straight. "Most of the arrests were for unlawful assembly," he says. "After a while we got smart and developed a rapport with the strikers. We'd walk along with them and talk. After a couple of days of that, the arrests decreased drastically." The cops and demonstrators at the Strip and Flamingo may have attained relative peace, but the strike dragged on.

On May 19, a leader of the Culinary Union's international headquarters warned the Nevada Resort Association hotel owners that if the strike weren't settled soon, "... the destruction of America's leading resort community is inevitable."

Apparently unimpressed, the NRA filed two lawsuits against the international. The first called for the restoration of the union's health and benefits package; the second charged that the union had violated the provisions of a 10-day no-strike agreement.

Whether the threats and lawsuits played any role in the negotiations is unknown, but four days later a tentative agreement was reached with the Culinary and Bartender unions. At the same time, meetings were scheduled between the Stagehands and Musicians locals and the NRA, and final accords were shortly reached.

Las Vegas had survived, and

remained one of America's leading resort destinations.

Attorney Tom Pitaro has represented the Culinary Union since 1989. In January 2003 he said: "Metro and the unions knew that the kinds of things that happened in 1984 and afterward couldn't be allowed to keep repeating themselves. Both sides got together and reached agreement on how these matters would be handled in the future, an arrangement that protected the rights of the members and did away with the violence of the past. The relationship between the police and the unions in Las Vegas today should be used as a model for cities across the nation."

Discrimination

In August 1984 Metro was the defendant in a lawsuit brought by minority employees, alleging that the department's minority-hiring practices did not reflect the makeup of the Las Vegas job market. The U.S. Justice Department argued that the number of ethnic and female staff was well below the ratio in the community in general. They wanted Metro to hire previously rejected minority applicants and pay them retroactively.

Metro countered that the department was open to all candidates who passed the educational, psychological, and physical tests and completed a 16-week course at the training academy. "We cannot sacrifice the safety of our community by hiring individuals who previously failed employment examinations," Sheriff Moran argued.

It took four years to resolve the issue via Consent Decree. The settlement called for a new type of entry-level examination, a change in the transfer policy, and an aggressive minority and female recruitment program.

PEAP

In an effort to help police officers deal with the emotional effects of traumatic experiences, such as officer-involved shootings, the Police Employee Assistance Program was established on September 22, 1984.

The efforts that led to the implementation of the PEAP program began in 1983 and were spearheaded by Lt. Jerry Keller and Detective Edward Jensen. Keller had been assigned to the Internal Affairs Bureau and dealt with citizen complaints of misconduct by officers. He'd come to believe that if police personnel who were having difficulties on the job were identified early enough, their problems could be overcome, in many cases, through awareness training.

Detective Jensen had personal experience with on-the-job trauma, having been involved in three separate shooting incidents. He felt it was critical that officers who were involved in shootings receive immediate emotional support at the scene. Joining forces, the two men pushed for an officer-support program and, after some initial resistance, were successful.

As Metro grew in size, it became apparent that there was a need for an even greater range of assistance for all employees, both sworn and civilian. Recently, three police officers and one civilian have staffed PEAP. They function as peer counselors in providing crisis intervention, emotional support,

and professional counseling referrals to all LVMPD employees and their immediate families. These services are provided for such issues as relationship and parenting problems, dealing with death or loss situations, post-traumatic stress, alcohol/chemical dependency, and job-performance problems.

The success of the program has led to requests from police agencies all around Nevada, as well as Kingman, Arizona, for assistance in providing training and support. As a sign of that success, it should be noted that national statistics show that three out of every five police officers involved in a shoot-

Motorcycle Officer Gunned Down

Marc Kahre joined the LVMPD on October 2, 1973. On October 11, 1988, the 34-year-old spotted a car wanted in connection with shots fired during a domestic incident. Officer Kahre tailed the vehicle while waiting for backup. The suspect stopped abruptly, jumped from

his car, and opened fire. One bullet struck Kahre in the forehead, killing him. A backup officer arrived almost simultaneously and returned fire. Although the suspect was struck five times, he was able to get back into his vehicle and flee the scene. When he became involved in a traffic accident a short time later, the suspect took his own life by shooting himself in the head.

A wife and two sons, ages 8 and 10, survived Officer Kahre.

ing leaves law enforcement within one year of the event. Since 1984, only one Metro officer is known to have resigned as a direct result of a shooting incident.

Career Criminals

In March 1988, the Repeat Offender Program (ROP) was established in the Career Criminal Section of the Detective Bureau. The purpose of this initiative was to identify and incarcerate the relatively small number of criminals who commit a large number of the crimes. The Criminal Apprehension Team (CAT) was added in January 1992. Their mission was to locate and apprehend fugitives wanted for felony violations of state and federal laws.

Lieutenant James Moses has been with Metro for 25 years and in the Career Criminal Section since 1997. He oversees the ROP and CAT, as well as the Fugitive Detail. In January 2003, he discussed the three units.

"We deal with the meanest of the mean, the worst of the worst," Moses said. "The officers who work these details are highly skilled and motivated. To keep it that way, I don't allow any dead weight. Anybody who doesn't want to hold up his end will find himself working somewhere else."

The ROP targets the 20% of the criminals who are responsible for 80% of the crime. According to Lt. Moses, "Some of these guys are regular one-man crime waves, committing five or six felonies a day." The offenses these individuals are accused of range from auto theft to burglary, grand larceny, robbery, and murder.

When not chasing those particular types of bad guys, ROP officers are sometimes pressed into service helping other units. In that role, they handled the surveillance of Sandy Murphy and Rick Tabish, the suspects in the 1998 murder of casino mogul Ted Binion, and made the actual arrests when warrants were issued.

There are 57 CAT operations nationwide. In 1999, the Las Vegas team made 863 felony arrests, more than double those of cities such as New York and Los Angeles.

"Las Vegas is a transient town, a cash town with millions of tourists passing through each year. It's not surprising that criminals figure this is an easy place to get lost in," Moses says. "Just take a look at the number of wanted persons who are either arrested here or were in Vegas at some point while they were on the run. Even several of the 9/11 hijackers spent some time here before they attacked."

For those reasons, the Fugitive Detail serves an important role for the people of the Vegas Valley and the entire country. In fact, their arrests are primarily of people wanted in other jurisdictions.

"These officers are hunters who prey on criminals," is how Lt. Moses describes the personnel assigned to the Fugitive Detail. In 2001, these "hunters" got 1,200 of the most wanted and most dangerous off the streets. In 2003, 1,180 felony arrests were made, including 85 for murder or attempted murder.

Controversial Death

At approximately 12:30 a.m. on July 31, 1990, three plainclothes Vice officers arrested a prostitute in the area of Paradise and Flamingo roads. Shortly after the arrest, they got permission from the suspect to enter the apartment she shared with a male friend. Suspecting he may have been functioning as a pimp, they wanted to question him about the exact nature of his relationship with the woman. Using a key allegedly voluntarily provided by the woman, the three officers entered the apartment at 4350 Paradise Road.

According to statements provided by the three officers, 39-year-old Charles Bush was apparently asleep in bed when they entered the bedroom. When he awakened, possibly startled by the presence of the three men, Bush leaped out of bed and charged one of the cops. The officer wrestled him to the floor and with the help of his two partners handcuffed the suspect and placed him on the bed. At that point it was noticed that Bush had stopped breathing. Paramedics were called, but the man was dead by the time they arrived.

However, Bush's girlfriend denied giving the cops the key to the apartment or permission to enter it. She questioned the police account of what happened at the residence and denied soliciting the officers for sex. She believed her arrest was baseless and the police raid on the apartment was illegal.

The three officers were eventually charged with Involuntary Manslaughter and Oppression Under the Color of Law in Bush's death. A subsequent trial ended in a hung jury, with acquittal favored by a count of 11 to 1. Based on those numbers, prosecutors declined to try the case again.

That wasn't the end of the story for the in-volved cops, however. All were subject to disciplinary action for violations of Metro policy and procedure. One officer retired before proceedings against him were commenced. The other two were sanctioned, but remained in the department.

Although there were no criminal convictions, the story had legs with the media and became a major source of adverse publicity for Metro. It was later cited by Undersheriff Eric Cooper as one of the reasons he decided not to run for sheriff.

Traffic Accident Claims Officer

On October 23, 1992, Officer Donald Weese responded to a call about a man with a gun. While en route, his car collided with another vehicle at Charleston and Eastern. Officer Weese sustained massive injuries and died at the scene.

He'd been on the force since September 11, 1990, and was 25 at the time of his death. Officer Weese's parents survived him.

Donald Weese

The Moran Era Ends

John Moran stepped down as sheriff in December 1994, at the end of his third term. He passed away in June 1998 at the age of 75.

Ray Sheffer and John Moran

4

The Mob's Man

Introduction

Anthony "Tony the Ant" Spilotro was born on May 19, 1938, in Chicago, Illinois, the fourth of six sons. Though born to honest Italian immigrants, Tony ran afoul of the law at an early age when he became involved in petty offenses, such as shoplifting and purse snatching. At a mere five-feet-six-inches tall, he became known as a tough kid with a "little-man's syndrome." After his father died, young Spilotro was thrown out of school in 1955 for roughing up teachers and fellow students. Taking to the streets, he fell in with other kids in the same boat and was soon involved with more serious crime. Tony developed a reputation as being totally ruthless, which was considered an asset in his line of work.

In the early 1960s, his abilities came to the attention of career criminal Sam "Mad Sam" DeStefano. Sam was in the loan-sharking business and had a gift for spotting street kids who were as depraved as he was. He put such people to work as enforcers to collect from borrowers who were slow in paying back their loans. Spilotro took to the job like a duck takes to water. He brought Mad Sam lots of "juice"—the ridiculously high weekly interest the debtor was charged. Although DeStefano was connected to the Chicago mob, he was not part of the organization's leadership. He did, however, give Spilotro an assignment that would bring the newcomer to the attention of the bosses.

In 1962, two thugs named Billy McCarthy and Jimmy Miraglia murdered three legitimate businessmen during a robbery attempt. Unfortunately for them, they committed the murders in a Chicago neighborhood where many of the mobsters lived. To avoid unwanted attention, the bosses declared the area off-limits when it came to murder. DeStefano asked Spilotro to track down the killers and make sure they never violated the rules again. In what would become known as the "M&M Murders," Tony located McCarthy, but not Miraglia. He questioned McCarthy, demanding that he turn in his partner. When McCarthy's cooperation proved to be less than enthusiastic, Spilotro put his captive's head in a vise and squeezed, then squeezed some more. The stubborn McCar-

thy resisted as long as he could, but after one of his eyes popped out, he decided to give up his pal. The bodies of McCarthy and Miraglia were later found in the trunk of an abandoned car.

Spilotro Moves to Las Vegas

After this successful debut, Spilotro became a soldier in the Chicago crime family. He was promoted to the position of capo (captain) in 1968. In 1971, he was sent to Las Vegas to help keep an eye on the mob's casino interests. Although nearly every organized-crime family nationwide was represented in Vegas, the Chicago organization was dominant. As such, Tony knew their representative in Sin City would have special clout. He knew that a street-smart man like himself could go beyond the casino skimming operations, at the time overseen by his old buddy Frank "Lefty" Rosenthal, and virtually have a piece of all the other organized criminal activities taking place in Vegas. Tony knew he could be "the Man" when it came to street crime. It was a position he wanted, and was his for the taking. Tony made his move and was equal to the task. For the next 15 years, he was the top dog among the criminal element in Las Vegas.

Frank Rosenthal was 10 years

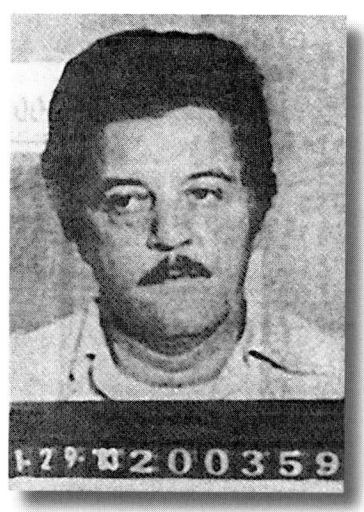

Tony Spilotro

Reign of Terror

A 1974 study by the *Los Angeles Times* showed that in the three years since Tony Spilotro arrived in Las Vegas, there had been more Mafia-style murders than in the prior 25 years combined. It didn't really matter whether or not Tony was responsible for them; casino insiders and federal and local authorities were convinced they were his doing. The little man's reputation grew rapidly, emboldening him even further. "Everybody on the Strip [is] scared to death of the little bastard," one casino owner was quoted as saying in a different *L.A. Times* article. "He struts in and out of the joints like Little Caesar."

older than Spilotro and was considered to be one of the premier oddsmakers in the country. The Chicago Crime Commission listed both Rosenthal and Spilotro as bona fide members of the Chicago crime syndicate. Rosenthal had arrived in Vegas in 1966 and quietly bought into a local sports book. Soon after that he became an executive at the Stardust Hotel, one of the mob's Strip properties. Lefty was being groomed to be the Chicago family's watchdog in Las Vegas. In addition to knowing Spilotro from Chicago, the two men had been in Miami together earlier in the '60s, when Rosenthal was running a bookmaking operation there. In Florida, Lefty was the boss and Tony was described as serving in a "gofer" capacity. The Miami endeavor had come to the attention of the FBI, which conducted extensive surveillance on Lefty and Tony. When the pair reunited in

Vegas, law-enforcement authorities assumed Spilotro's role would again be as Rosenthal's flunky. This assumption turned out to be a major miscalculation.

After settling into town, Spilotro opened a jewelry and gift concession at the Circus Circus casino. He ran the store using the name of Anthony Stuart—Stuart being his wife's maiden name—doing business as Anthony Stuart, Ltd. Jewelry concessions in casinos were generally hard to come by unless a person had clout; in this case Spilotro and Rosenthal seemed to have plenty with Circus Circus owner, Jay Sarno. Although it was against Nevada gaming regulations for a casino to do business with anyone having ties to organized crime, Sarno's nearly $20 million in loans from the Chicago-based Teamster Pension Fund apparently ensured he'd disregard that rule.

The Anthony Stuart alias initially gave Spilotro a chance to check out the potential for other criminal enterprises in Las Vegas relatively free from the close scrutiny he would later be under. It didn't take long for the Ant to realize that Vegas was an ideal location for something he was already well-schooled in: loan sharking. The population in the Vegas Valley was at about 300,000 then, with more people flocking in every day. Many of these folks worked in the casinos as dealers, valets, cleaners, and food servers. They relied heavily on tips as part of their pay, and tips weren't guaranteed. Even for someone making pretty good money, Vegas was a 24-hour action town where cash could be hard to come by, but easily let go of. Frequently, a local needed a little financial help to make it through to the next payday. It was indeed a dream situation for a guy like Tony Spilotro.

Spilotro Beats a Murder Rap

Things turned a bit rocky for Tony the following year, however. According to a 1983 *Los Angeles Times* article, it all started in August 1972 when Sgt. Charles Lee of the Clark County Sheriff's Department, who had previously been a Chicago cop, received a phone call from a Chicago homicide detective he knew. Lee was told that a Cook County, Illinois, grand jury had issued a murder indictment against Spilotro, Mad Sam DeStefano, and his brother Mario for the 1963 torture and killing of a Chicago loan shark named Leo Foreman. Two Chicago detectives were flying to Las Vegas that night to arrest Spilotro and they wanted a couple of local officers along as backup.

The next words Sgt. Lee heard were chilling: "Chuck, you're the only guy I trust. Our snitches on the street here say you've got a leak down there—one of your boys is on the mob's payroll. Be careful."

Lee reported the call to a superior and two trusted officers were assigned to work with the Chicago detectives. Tony Spilotro was arrested without incident and booked into the jail to await extradition proceedings. After the arresting officers left, the jail was placed under covert surveillance to see if Spilotro received any assistance from local law enforcement.

Sure enough, a 32-year-old officer named John DeMoss of the Organized Crime and Homicide unit signed into the jail with his niece, saying that he wanted to give her a tour of the facility. Once inside, he stopped at Spilotro's cell. After speaking with the inmate, DeMoss contacted an attorney for Tony, delivered a message to him from Rosenthal, and began making arrangements for bail.

DeMoss was confronted by department brass and resigned. He wouldn't be unemployed for long, though. Almost immediately, he was hired as a supervisor at Lefty Rosenthal's Stardust. The ex-cop was later named as a suspect in gangland killings in Nevada and California, but was never arrested.

Starting in September, Tony Spilotro, having been released on $10,000 bail, shuttled back and forth between Chicago and Las Vegas. By doing so, he was able to assist in trial preparation in the Windy City and take care of his business interests in Nevada.

One thing bothering Tony on the Chicago front was that he was being tried with Mad Sam, who planned to act as his own attorney. More troubling, though, was that Sam had cancer and rumors were circulating that he was considering making a deal for a lighter sentence to avoid dying in prison. A requirement for any such arrangement would be that Sam turn on his brother Mario and the Ant. Tony had his attorney try to sever his case from DeStefano's, but failed. He next appealed to Chicago's top mobster, Tony Accardo, complaining that Mad Sam was sure to take a fall and would take him down, too.

Five weeks before the trial, someone fired two shotgun blasts into Mad Sam's chest. An infor-

mant later fingered Mario DeStefano and Spilotro for the hit, but no charges were ever filed and Sam's murder remained unsolved. In June 1973, Spilotro was acquitted in the murder of Leo Foreman.

Although he got off the hook in Chicago, Tony Spilotro had lost something in the process: his low profile. His case had received a lot of publicity and he was now in the harsh glare of the law-enforcement spotlight.

Spilotro Digs In

By 1975, Spilotro needed a new headquarters. His entourage had increased several-fold with the arrival of his brother, John, and the influx of bookies, loan sharks, and

John Spilotro

other heavies from Chicago. Still using the name of Anthony Stuart, he set up shop in the card room at the Dunes, another casino in debt to the Teamster Pension Fund.

Nevada gaming officials quickly intervened, however. Privately and unofficially, they warned Major Riddle and Morris Shenker, owners of the Dunes, that they were placing their licenses in jeopardy by allowing Spilotro to operate out of their facility. The gangster agreed to find other pastures. The very next night, John Spilotro showed up at the Dunes. Using the name of John Adams, he fielded calls and met with the same cast of characters as brother Tony. It was pretty much business as usual and in a few weeks Tony Spilotro himself returned to the scene.

The following year, gaming officials took a more formal approach in their efforts to rid the Dunes of Tony Spilotro: They convened a hearing at which Riddle and Shenker were asked to explain the gangster's continued presence on their property.

Riddle testified first, claiming that he had only recently learned Tony's last name was Spilotro and that he allegedly had organized-crime connections. Riddle said that he had questioned Tony about lending out money on the premises. Spilotro readily admitted to it, but said he never charged any interest on the loans. Riddle concluded that Tony was simply a "good-hearted person."

Morris Shenker was under oath next. No stranger to legal proceedings, the highly successful criminal-defense lawyer had represented many of the nation's major crime figures before the Kefauver Committee in the 1950s and was chief defense counsel for Teamster boss James Hoffa in the 1960s. In spite of his reputation as sharp and savvy, Shenker said he, too, was ignorant of Spilotro's true identity and character. Now that the matter had been brought to his attention, he vowed the gangster would be ejected from the Dunes and that should Spilotro ever return, he wouldn't waste any time in ousting him for good.

While the Dunes' owners were proclaiming the end of Tony Spilotro's presence on their turf, the Ant had already arranged an even better deal. He took up residence in the exclusive Las Vegas Country Club and Estates, a walled residential and recreational complex complete with guard posts at the entrances. It was a place that authorities would find difficult to penetrate to initiate personal or electronic surveillance.

There was a brief time of distress for Tony when the Membership Committee of the community denied his application. However, after Frank Rosenthal and other of

Spilotro's influential acquaintances spoke on his behalf, the Committee realized their error and admitted Tony and one of his lieutenants. The snub was soon forgotten and the Spilotros became a part of the group; his wife, Nancy, was a regular sight on the tennis courts.

Always looking to improve his situation, it wasn't long before Tony found what must have seemed like a panacea. He moved his business operations to yet another location, opening the Gold Rush jewelry store on West Sahara, a block from the Strip. The two-story building was equipped with a buzzer-operated entrance door and Tony had a private security company "sweep" the place periodically, looking for electronic bugs. The upper floor contained five police scanners to monitor local and federal law-enforcement activities, as well as two sophisticated radio transmitters and receivers for communication with associates without using telephones. Spotters with binoculars sometimes stationed themselves on the roof or in cars parked nearby, searching for any sign of police surveillance. Tony, his brother John, and Herbert "Fat Herbie" Blitzstein, a 300-pound convicted bookie from Chicago, ran the store. A loaded 9mm semi-automatic and a .45 revolver were kept under the counter should unwanted guests show up. When the FBI subsequently raided the store, agents stated in sworn affidavits that the Gold Rush was a "veritable warehouse of stolen property" and more than 70% of its inventory came from a nationwide burglary and fencing ring.

Hole in the Wall Gang

Some of the people responsible for the presence of stolen goods in the Gold Rush were Tony Spilotro's personal crew of burglars, called the "Hole in the Wall Gang," a group usually consisting of five members. The name came from their practice of cutting a hole in the wall of a targeted business in order to gain access. They didn't confine their criminal efforts only to commercial buildings, however. They hit residences with equal relish.

"These guys loved to steal. They could have ten grand in their pocket and they'd go out and steal a pack of gum, just for the sake of stealing something," a veteran Metro detective said of the gang in a 2003 interview. In addition to being avid thieves, some of the crew were also killers.

"I know that one guy, who's now in prison in another state, killed at least nine people across the country. I was part of an undercover operation that helped put him away. When he was in court for sentencing, he said that if he ever got out he'd come back and get my family and me. I believe him," the same detective said.

Spilotro had more sources of revenue than what his efforts produced directly. He had attained such a position of prominence in the criminal world that anyone else wanting to run an illegal operation in Vegas required his permission. This included approving other burglary rings, or "hits" that were to be carried out locally. Another long-time detective cited one example. Valet parking attendants at one of the big Strip hotels ran a very successful operation. They became familiar with the identities of wealthy locals who visited the hotel for parties, shows, or just a night out for dinner and to do some gambling. When the victim dropped off his car, they'd ask how long he planned to be on the premises, implying that they had long- and short-term parking areas. If the person planned a long night, the car would be turned over to a burglar who would drive to the victim's residence. Armed with keys to the house or the garage door opener, he conducted a leisurely burglary. Of course, Spilotro had to be paid a 'street tax'—a kick-

Hole in the Wall Gang behind bars

back—in return for allowing the burglars to stay in business."

The Cop Connection

In addition to managing his criminal operations, Tony Spilotro spent time and effort in collecting information on what his enemies— police and federal agents—were up to. He had the scanners to monitor law-enforcement activities, but someone had to tell him what crystals he needed in order to listen in on all their frequencies, including highly secret surveillance channels. Tony found a couple of people who could not only provide that information, but also give him other first-hand intelligence. Metro Detective Joe Blasko and Sgt. Philip Leone both held sensitive positions in the department's anti-crime operations. They often reported directly to Sheriff Ralph Lamb. In time they reported to both Lamb and Tony Spilotro.

Later, when Spilotro's phones were tapped and his home and offices bugged, agents taped the two officers giving information to Spilotro or other mobsters about upcoming raids and the identities of undercover operatives. When this information came to light in 1978, Leone retired and moved to New Jersey. Joe Blasko was fired and went to work full-time for Spilotro. Both men were subsequently indicted for their activities while employed as police officers, but neither was ever tried. The charges against Leone were dropped because of the defendant's health problems. Blasko was not pursued for evidentiary reasons. Afterward, he was convicted of crimes he committed while employed directly by Tony Spilotro and served five years in state and federal prisons.

LVMPD Goes After Spilotro

In January 1979, John McCarthy was sworn in as Clark County Sheriff. In one of his first actions, he appointed Detective Kent Clifford to command the department's intelligence unit. Simultaneously, he declared war on organized crime, specifically the Spilotro gang. Clifford didn't hold his prey in very

high esteem. "Spilotro was a killer and he was dangerous, but he was just a street punk. That's all he ever was," Clifford said.

Early in McCarthy's tenure, Metro moved to improve the relationship with its FBI counterparts. Both agencies had suffered previously from adverse publicity over real and alleged incidents of corruption in dealing with the mob. In a March 2003 interview, Kent Clifford stated that the fight against Spilotro and his cohorts required an all-out effort, involving local and federal law enforcement and the public. "In order to win, we needed to all work together. There had to be cooperation between law enforcement and the public had to support us."

The cooperation between the locals and feds did seem to flourish under McCarthy's leadership. Both agencies recognized the danger posed by the gangsters and the need to defeat them. It was somewhat more difficult to excite the public, however, because the vast majority didn't feel they were directly affected by mob activities. Most of the murders taking place were criminal-on-criminal acts, which didn't inflame the average citizen. However, even if it wasn't a priority for them, the public did support the police efforts.

Over the next four years, the law's battles with the criminals seemed more appropriate appearing in a Hollywood production than a history book. It was an exciting time to be a cop in Las Vegas.

Tony, Geri, and Lefty

In early 1980, Tony Spilotro made one of several major mistakes that eventually contributed to his fall from grace with his superiors in Chicago: He became romantically involved with another man's wife. It wasn't simply a fling with some unknown dame looking for a thrill. The woman was none other than Geri Rosenthal, Lefty's 44-year-old wife. Many of the details of the illicit relationship were depicted in the movie *Casino*, starring Joe Pesci, Robert De Niro, and Sharon Stone.

Geri arrived in Vegas from California in the late 1950s. She performed as a topless showgirl at the Tropicana and Dunes for a while, then worked as a cocktail waitress. In 1968, she met the recently arrived Frank Rosenthal. Lefty immediately fell head-over-heels for Geri; they were married the following year.

Initially, things seemed to be going well for Lefty and Geri. He was a powerful casino executive and she was enjoying a free-spending lifestyle. By 1973 she had given birth to their second child, Stephanie. Both Stephanie and her older brother Stephen were natural swimmers. The kids became members of the Las Vegas Sandpipers swim team. The proud parents spent many hours working with their offspring in the family pool on hot desert afternoons. They attended all swim tournaments and Lefty served as the official announcer, except for the races that Stephen and Stephanie competed in. They were the kind of family, living the kind of life, most Americans would envy, or so it appeared.

Lefty had other things on his mind besides kids and swimming, however. He was locked in a battle with the Nevada Gaming Control Board, which was trying to have him barred from casino operations because of his relationship with Spilotro. It was a fight the oddsmaker lost in 1978, forcing him into retirement. Rosenthal later called the decision a "blessing in disguise," allowing him to devote more time to his children. In spite of the professional setback, Lefty Rosenthal remained upbeat.

That wasn't the case with Geri. Beneath the surface, she was seething. Increasingly dependent on alcohol and drugs, she frequently went out in the evening and didn't come home until dawn. The relationship between her and her husband deteriorated.

Then, in early 1980, Geri publicly exposed her adulterous

relationship. She appeared in two of her favorite haunts, a health club and a beauty salon, all decked out in a new mink coat and diamond ring. In response to the "ooohs" and "ahhhs," Geri made no secret of the source of the coat and ring: Tony Spilotro. She explained that he was her "sponsor." On the street, that meant Spilotro was her boyfriend and protector.

"Spilotro openly flaunted his relationship with Geri as a show of power," former police Commander Kent Clifford said. "He could have had dozens of women, younger and prettier. It was a stupid thing to do."

The situation reached critical mass on September 8, 1980. Geri Rosenthal arrived home at 9 a.m. after staying out all night, likely high on booze, drugs, or both. Finding herself locked out of her house, she became hysterical. Getting back into her Mercedes, she repeatedly rammed the car into Lefty's parked Cadillac. All the noise brought her husband from the house, and several neighbors came out onto their lawns in bathrobes and pajamas. A security guard called the police.

As two Metro officers arrived, Spilotro and his wife, Nancy, showed up. Geri was in a screaming match with Lefty, threatening that she just might accommodate the FBI, which wanted to talk to her. After making that announcement, she pulled a pearl-handled revolver from her blouse and aimed it in the general direction of her husband's head. According to the police report, she shouted: "My sponsor is Tony Spilotro and what are you going to do about that?"

At that point the officers drew their weapons and took cover behind their car, but the five-foot 97-pound Nancy Spilotro charged the "other woman," wrestled her to the ground, and disarmed her.

With the immediate danger over and additional police units on the scene, Geri said she was leaving for the bank where the Rosenthals kept three safe-deposit boxes. She asked the police officers to escort her. Geri led the unique caravan in her Mercedes; the police cars followed, while Lefty brought up the rear in his damaged Caddy. Inside the bank, Geri cleaned out the safe-deposit boxes, reportedly containing $200,000 in cash and a million dollars worth of jewelry. While she completed the looting, the police were keeping Lefty at bay outside. With her banking business done, Geri jumped back into her car and took off at a fairly high rate of speed, in the direction of California.

The FBI and Metro detectives later located her and asked for her cooperation in their investigations of Lefty and Tony. She refused, allegedly confiding to friends that someone had contacted her and suggested it might be a good idea for her to keep her mouth shut.

Not even the proceeds from the safe-deposit boxes could make a happy life for Geri, though. At 4:30 a.m. on November 6, 1982, she stumbled into the office of a seedy Sunset Boulevard motel. She started screaming, then collapsed unconscious to the floor. She was transported to a hospital, but never came out of the coma. The medical examiner ruled her death an accident: a lethal combination of cocaine, Valium, and other drugs. What happened to the money and valuables she had when she left Las Vegas remains a mystery.

As for Lefty, he had survived a 25-year association with the mob and gotten out of it healthy and wealthy. In spite of the shattering end of his marriage, things weren't all that bad for him, at least not until the night of October 4, 1982. He left one of his favorite hangouts—Tony Roma's restaurant on Sahara—around 8:30 and got into his 1981 Cadillac. When he turned the ignition key, he got a little more than the usual purr of the engine he was expecting. Someone had placed a charge of C-4 explosive under the trunk next to the gas tank and wired it to the ignition. He should have been killed instantly, but a steel plate under the driver's seat, standard equipment in all Cadillacs, diverted the blast toward the pas-

Lefty Rosenthal's Cadillac

senger side, blowing the roof 60 feet into the air. Miraculously, Rosenthal was able to get away from the car before the gas tank exploded. He was taken to the hospital with only minor injuries.

The Las Vegas cops and the FBI figured the incident might loosen Lefty's tongue, and both agencies approached him with offers of protection in return for information. Rosenthal turned them both down. He moved out of Las Vegas shortly afterward. No one was ever charged in the attempt on his life.

Tony Spilotro seemed to have come out the winner, but his apparent lack of judgment in getting involved with Geri Rosenthal had come to the attention of his bosses in Chicago. They were unimpressed and soon became even more disenchanted.

The Bluestein Affair

While the drama in the personal lives of the Rosenthals and Spilotros played out, the Ant and the cops continued to engage in their own war. On the night of June 9, 1980, two Metro detectives were staking out one of the Spilotro gang's meeting places, the Upper Crust pizza parlor and the adjoining My Place bar at Flamingo Road and Maryland Parkway. Spilotro and some of his associates were in the pizza shop. For Detectives Gene Smith and David Groover, it had all the makings of another tedious shift of surveillance, until the 1979 Lincoln with Illinois plates pulled in.

Groover had been working the Spilotro investigation for a long time and was intimately familiar with the Ant and his operations. "We put in a lot of long boring hours sitting on those guys, but there were some exciting moments, too," Groover said in March 2003. "One time we tried to attach a tracking device under one of their vehicles. The guy's car was in a restaurant parking lot. My partner was under the car when the guy comes out of the restaurant unexpectedly and gets behind the wheel. I figured he was going to at least discover my partner, if not run him over. After a few tense seconds, the guy got out of the car and went back into the restaurant. To this day, I don't know why he came out; we were just damn glad he didn't drive away. The next day, we're following him and he pulls into a garage for an oil change. As soon as the mechanic got the car up on the hoist he spotted the bug and pointed it out to the subject. He and his lawyer went downtown and raised hell about police harassment."

Regarding the events of June 9, Groover remembers it this way: "This Lincoln with Illinois plates pulled in and the driver went into the Upper Crust. We weren't familiar with the vehicle and were curious as to who the new player was. The guy talked with Spilotro and Frank Cullotta for a while and obviously wasn't a casual customer. When he left, we decided to follow him and see if we could get a better handle on who he was.

"As soon as he pulled out on Flamingo he started speeding, doing eighty or better, and driving recklessly. I was driving and stayed close behind. Eventually we decided we had enough probable cause on the traffic violations to pull the car over and check him out. By that time we were on McLeod near a new development called Sunrise Villas and the driver had slowed to normal speed. We put the red light on the dash and activated it. The Lincoln turned on Engresso, the street running into the development, went past an unmanned security booth, and stopped several yards beyond. I got out of out unmarked car and approached the Lincoln, verbally identifying myself as a police officer and displaying my badge."

Groover and Smith weren't aware at the time that the Lincoln was being driven by Frank Bluestein, also known as Frank Blue, a 35-year-old maitre d' at the Hacienda Hotel and Casino. Bluestein lived with his girlfriend in the Sunrise Villas. His father, Steve Bluestein, was an official with the local Culinary Union and had been the subject of a 1978 search warrant as part of the FBI investigation of Anthony Spilotro.

"When I got part way to the Lincoln, the car pulled away at a slow speed," Groover continued the story. "I got back in our car and followed. The guy pulled over again a short distance down the road. I angled our car toward his and got out of the car again, approaching the other vehicle while identifying myself. This time my partner got out, too, and took up a position by our passenger door.

"The driver of the Lincoln lowered his window, but didn't say anything. All of a sudden, Gene hollered, 'Dave, he's got a gun! He's got a gun!' I retreated back behind my car door. Gene and I continued to yell at the guy that we were cops and to put down his gun. He never said a word, but instead of getting rid of his weapon, he turned slightly in his seat and aimed the gun at Gene. Assuming he intended to shoot, Gene and I both opened fire."

Bluestein was struck several times and died at a nearby hospital a couple of hours later. To the Bluestein family, Tony Spilotro, and their attorney Oscar Goodman, the death of Frank Bluestein was not a legitimate use of deadly force. Far from it. Allegations flew that the maitre d' had been executed and the cops planted a gun on him to justify the murder.

"There was a real firestorm over that deal," Groover recalls. "We traced the gun Bluestein had to one of his brothers, pretty much destroying the planted-gun allegations being put forth. We didn't release that information to the press right away, though. We waited until the inquest to make it public."

Less than two weeks later, a coroner's jury ruled the death of Frank Bluestein a "justifiable homicide." The cops were okay in that regard, but the ruling didn't prevent the filing of numerous civil lawsuits, including a $22 million federal case alleging the police had violated Frank Bluestein's civil rights. The suit dragged on for five years before being decided in favor of the cops.

The courts are the legal mechanism for people seeking redress of perceived wrongs and the courts were used in the Bluestein matter. However, if a person doesn't trust that system or feels the potential penalties are insufficient, there are other means of justice, "illegal justice," that can be found for the right price. Someone, possibly the Bluestein family, decided to use the latter route to exact revenge on detectives Smith and Groover. A contract was put out on the two cops and, because of his lofty posi-

tion, Tony Spilotro had to have approved the death warrants.

David Groover, Gene Smith, and Kent Clifford each believe to this day that the Bluesteins were behind the attempt to have the officers killed. They further agree that the effort must have had the knowledge and blessing of Tony Spilotro. This would prove to be another error in judgment by the Las Vegas kingpin. The mob tries to best the law by outwitting or corrupting, not by killing. The murder of cops draws a lot of heat and attention. The last thing Chicago wanted was heat and attention focused on their lucrative Vegas operations. His bosses were soon to learn that the Ant was running amok.

Clifford Backs Down the Mob

Kent Clifford remembers first hearing about the murder contracts and his reaction. "For quite a while after the coroner's inquest, there was some sniping between the Bluestein lawyers and the department, and the filing of some civil actions. I thought that was all that was going on. And then I get this call from an informant we had inside Spilotro's gang. He tells me a hit man from Chicago is in town to do Smith and Groover. The guy came in by way of Denver, where he picked up some clean weapons for the job.

"I went berserk. Spilotro knew my goal was to put him in prison for the rest of his life; I'd told him that more than once. We were adversaries, but there were certain rules we played by. You didn't put out contracts on cops, and even if Tony didn't actually order the job, he damn sure knew about it. I decided that Chicago would never have authorized a move like that and they probably didn't know what Spilotro was up to. I decided to take a chance and visit Chicago in person to straighten things out."

In March 1981, Clifford and his partner flew to Chicago with guns in their briefcases. They checked into a motel and were on the road in a rental car early the next morning. Their first stop was at the house of Joseph "Doves" Aiuppa, one of Spilotro's superiors.

"Aiuppa wasn't home when we arrived. Only his wife was there and she wouldn't let us in. I told her it was very important that I talk with her husband. I left her the phone number of our hotel and asked her to make sure he called me," Clifford said.

"Our next visit was to the home of Joseph 'Joey the Clown' Lombardo, another mob boss. He wasn't home either, but his wife invited us into the house and we talked for about ten minutes. We left the same message with her as with Mrs. Aiuppa. From there we stopped at

Tony Accardo's; he was out, too. Three stops and three misses."

Getting frustrated, Clifford and his partner remembered the name of a mob associate from Chicago whom they'd spotted visiting Spilotro in Vegas on occasion. They called the local FBI office and asked for information on Allen Dorfman. The feds said Dorfman was an insurance broker with known ties to the mob and provided his business address.

"When we got to Dorfman's office, I walked past the reception desk looking for him. The secretary said I couldn't do that and I told her to watch me. I guess it was quite an entrance. Anyway, we got to see Dorfman and I explained the situation to him. He said to go back to the hotel and someone would be in touch.

"That afternoon a lawyer who represented the mobsters called. I ran the whole scenario by him and requested a personal meeting with his clients. He said he'd talk to them and get back to me. He called back awhile later and said there would be a meeting that evening, but I wasn't invited. Although that didn't make me happy, there wasn't much I could do about it. I told the lawyer to relay a message to his clients just like I gave it to him. I said, 'If you kill my cops, I will bring forty men back here and kill everything that moves, walks, or crawls around all the houses I visited today. And that is not a threat, but a promise.' The lawyer said he'd deliver my message just like I said it. If the contracts were lifted, he told me I'd get a phone call with the message, 'Have a safe journey home, Commander.' If I didn't receive a call, 'then all bets are off.'

"I dozed off and around two a.m., the phone rang. I'm not sure of the identity of the caller, but the message was for me to have a safe journey home. The contracts were lifted." Clifford had accomplished what he'd gone to Chicago to do.

Not long after, Allen Dorfman was gunned down in what appeared to be a gangland hit. As far as is known, his murder had nothing to do with Spilotro or Clifford's visit.

Back in Las Vegas, Clifford thought it would be a return to business as usual. It was, until a few days later someone fired several shotgun blasts into the homes of Tony and John Spilotro. The police were blamed for the incidents. Clifford contacted Spilotro's attorney Oscar Goodman and asked for a face-to-face with Tony and John. The meeting was held in Goodman's office.

"Tony snarled at me and said: 'Commander, you went to Chicago and told them you have forty men. I want you to know I have four hundred men.' I looked directly at

him and said, 'That makes us even, doesn't it?' He stared at me with a questioning look on his face. 'How do you figure?' he asked. I told him that my men were all police trained and many were Vietnam veterans. Each one was worth ten of his street punks.

"I then told Tony that my men had not done the shooting at John's or his house and that we were not out to kill him or anyone else. He accused me of making a statement on TV that I was going to kill him. What he was talking about happened after charges against him of being in the Sahara while he was in the 'black book' were dropped. Outside of the courtroom, I said to a reporter that there would be another day. Tony took that to mean that since I hadn't gotten him in court, I was going to kill him. He probably thought that because that's the way he did business. I clarified that my statement meant I planned to put him in prison, because that would be better justice than killing him. When I left that meeting, it was understood that the personal stuff was over and things would be back to normal."

The End of Spilotro

The next major highlight occurred on July 4, 1981. With businesses closed and most people involved in holiday festivities,

Spilotro's burglars decided to pay a call on Bertha's furniture and jewelry store in the 800 block of East Sahara. On this job the gang consisted of six men; three went on the roof to break in, while Joe Blasko and two others remained on watch at street level.

To the crooks, everything seemed to be going without a hitch. Unknown to them at the time, they'd been under police surveillance when they headed out for Bertha's and their activities had been videotaped from an adjoining roof. The Hole in the Wall Gang got nailed in he act and was whisked away to jail. On the surface, it didn't seem like that big a deal at all. Certainly nothing that would help to topple the mighty Tony Spilotro and other organized-crime figures from across the country. After all, crooks got arrested every day. And these guys had all been around the block before and knew the ropes. But according to many informed insiders, it marked the beginning of the end of organized-crime's dominance in Las Vegas.

One of the six men arrested

Michael Spilotro

that day was named Frank Cullotta. A long-time member of the Chicago mob and a friend of Spilotro's, Cullotta had served time and wasn't particularly anxious to go back for more. On top of that, he was the number-one suspect in an open murder case. Kent Clifford and his men decided Cullotta might be a good man to lean on a little bit. It proved to be a very wise move.

After Metro detectives made some positive gains, the FBI joined the ongoing negotiations with Cullotta. Eventually, they reached a deal. The former Spilotro lieutenant would talk in return for a break on sentencing for his current charges relating to the Hole in the Wall Gang, immunity from other crimes admitted, and placement in the federal Witness Protection Program for himself and his family.

In May 1982, the fact that Cullotta was cooperating was announced publicly. Oscar Goodman, speaking on behalf of his client, said Tony Spilotro wished Cullotta the best. Goodman wasn't worried about the former associate saying anything detrimental about

Tony, because there was nothing detrimental to say.

The facts were quite different, however. Cullotta had information leading back to Chicago and crime families in other cities, as well as the dirt on what was going on in Las Vegas.

To add to Spilotro's woes and those of his associates, the FBI continued to amass reel after reel of tapes obtained from tapping Tony's phones and other bugs. The little man was quite a talker and he liked to toot his own horn—yet another trait his bosses didn't take kindly to.

As time passed, Frank Cullotta talked to the cops. So did Tony Spilotro, only he didn't realize it. Indictments began to be handed up. Even though Kent Clifford was no longer with Metro, having left the department after a change of sheriffs in 1983, the ball he'd started rolling under Sheriff McCarthy maintained momentum under the new administration. Mobsters across the country were making court appearances and spending a lot of money on legal fees.

In 1986, the Chicago outfit had a new boss, Joe Ferriola. After getting his house in order, he summoned the embattled Spilotro back to Chicago. On June 14, Tony and his brother Michael, also a mob member, were told they were needed at a strategy meeting with one of Ferriola's top aides. The meeting was to take place in a cornfield on a farm in St. Anne, Indiana. The Spilotros went to the meeting, but never returned. A farmer discovered the grave containing their badly beaten bodies. Autopsies determined that both men, although severely injured, had been alive at the time they were buried. No charges were filed in their murders. Tony Spilotro, the mob's man in Las Vegas, was gone.

The End of the Spilotro Era

The last remnant of the Spilotro era survived until January 6, 1997. On that date, Herb "Fat Herbie" Blitzstein was found dead in his Las Vegas townhouse, shot in the back of the head.

After Spilotro's murder, Blitzstein had continued to do some loan sharking and handle stolen property. Convicted on federal charges, he served time in prison until 1991. After being released, he returned to Vegas and resumed his career.

The police theory of the murder was that members of the Los Angeles and Buffalo organized-crime families wanted to take over Herb's businesses and hired a contract killer to get Blitzstein out of the way.

That April, two Las Vegas men with ties to the Los Angeles

and Buffalo mobs were indicted for hiring people to kill Blitzstein and other racketeering-related charges. Two years later, both men were acquitted of the murder charges, but were convicted of running an extortion scheme to take over Herbie's loan-sharking and insurance-fraud operations. The two hit men who actually carried out the murder were arrested and both entered guilty pleas prior to going to trial.

The reign of Tony Spilotro had it all: sex and money, hit contracts and corrupt cops, shootouts and murders. Most of the main players from both sides are now either dead, in jail, or retired. Although they're gone, they will forever remain a part of Las Vegas history.

Herb Blitzstein

5

Civil Unrest 1992

Westside Story

Introduction

On March 3, 1991, police in Los Angeles attempted to stop a car for a traffic violation. The operator of the vehicle refused to comply and a pursuit ensued. When the automobile was finally pulled over, the driver—a black male named Rodney King—disobeyed the orders of the arresting officers. A scuffle followed, 81 seconds of which were captured on videotape by an uninvolved spectator. The video showed the officers delivering 56 blows on King, in addition to the use of taser darts, in an effort to get the suspect under control. The tape was shown repeatedly on national television.

The beating of Rodney King resulted in a public outcry for the police to be held accountable for what appeared to be a clear case of excessive use of force. Four LAPD officers were eventually charged for their roles in the incident. To the astonishment of many, on April 29, 1992, a jury in Simi Valley, California, acquitted the officers of the most serious charges. The verdicts sparked outrage in the black community.

The violence that followed became known as the "Rodney King riots." They began in Los Angeles: days of arson, looting, and assaults that tore the city apart. But although Los Angeles was the epicenter, other cities also felt the repercussions of the verdicts in the King case. One of those cities was Las Vegas.

It Couldn't Happen Here, But Just in Case ...

Word of the jury's decision in the King trial, and the reaction to it, began reaching the streets of Las Vegas that afternoon. As a precautionary measure, Sheriff John Moran instructed the LVMPD Field Services Division to develop a contingency plan to deal with any civil unrest that might develop locally as a result of the verdicts.

The department hierarchy didn't anticipate problems, however; Las Vegas' economy was better than Los Angeles'. Also, the minority community was too sophisticated to resort to such tactics and Metro's relationship with them was good, they reasoned.

Sheriff Moran contacted Lt. Steve Franks at the Northwest Area Command, which covered the predominantly black Westside. He advised him of the King verdicts and asked that his people be sensitive to the concerns of Westside residents. He also requested that Franks prepare an operational plan specific to Westside, in the event any problems arose there. As part of this plan, Sheriff Moran wanted officers to interact with the Westside community, walk foot patrol, and talk and listen to the populace.

The officers who worked Westside swing and graveyard shifts the night of April 29 found a community concerned and outraged over the verdicts, but willing to discuss the situation with the police.

While the evening was passing in relative peace in Las Vegas, Lt. Franks watched the violence in Los Angeles on television. The next morning he finalized his civil-unrest operational plan. It called for problem areas to be isolated and the trouble contained in the smallest geographical area possible; the LVMPD would take the offensive and only withdraw from an area to protect officer lives; priority would be placed on the safety of personnel and citizens, while defending property would be a secondary concern.

Lieutenant Franks briefed his superiors on the operational plan. He notified appropriate units and contacted the other two area commands, asking that they each have two squads available to assist should trouble appear. As the morning of April 30 passed, there was still no reason to think that Westside was about to explode.

The First Day of Violence

The first unusual incident occurred at noon at the Big 8 Market in the Nucleus Shopping Center at H Street and Owens Avenue. The driver of a truck delivering bottled water—a white male—was attacked by a group of approximately eight black males and beaten with hands, feet, and clubs. When the police arrived, the crowd that had formed around the beating incident fled into the nearby Sherman Gardens Housing Development. In spite of his injuries, the delivery driver declined to sign a complaint and said he'd seek his own medical treatment.

A short time later another fight call came in from the Big 8. Several officers responded and found that three males—two white and one Hispanic—who were doing plumbing and electrical work on the building had been beaten by a group of black males. The suspects, who had remained at the scene, were detained and questioned. They said the victims were beaten because they were white and weren't wanted in the neighborhood.

As with the delivery driver, these victims did not want to prosecute. To avoid further inflaming the situation, the suspects were released.

Over the next several hours, the calls for police response coming into the Communications Center increased dramatically in volume and violence. Although these incidents were primarily limited to Westside, there were occurrences in other areas as well. In addition to these concerns, a Housing Authority officer reported seeing an unusually high number of gang members on the streets of Westside. He warned that uniformed officers should "watch their backs."

LVMPD Jurisdiction

Incidents of violence continued to escalate. Several black males at D Street and Owens accosted a white female motorist; she was beaten and her car vandalized. The suspects all vanished before the police arrived.

At 2 p.m. a citizen reported several gang members gathered at a residence on North M Street with weapons and drugs. They were allegedly planning to get high and assault a police officer.

When officers arrived at the location, approximately 10 subjects fled and a foot pursuit ensued. Two people were subsequently arrested—one for possession of narcotics and another for obstructing. As the suspects were being taken into custody, a TV news crew arrived and began filming. With the camera rolling, one of the arrestees being placed into a patrol car yelled that he was being beaten and began to struggle; he pleaded for help. He attempted to kick the officers and the windows in the vehicle.

A group of about 50 people gathered around the scene and started throwing rocks and bottles at the police vehicles. As the cops left the area, they encouraged the news people to leave with them; they refused. A short time later the crowd turned on the reporters and the police had to return to extract them.

By 3 p.m. the situation was deteriorating rapidly. Additional supervisors rushed to the Northwest Station; an Administrative Command Post was established and more officers were called in.

While awaiting the arrival of additional manpower, Lt. Franks drove into Westside to personally evaluate the situation. He found that although incidents were increasing, they seemed to be scattered and unorganized. The obscenities, rocks, and bottles hurled at his car, however, were an omen of things to come. Darkness was descending on Las Vegas and what would become known as Fright Night was about to begin.

Combat Conditions

Ten years after the incident, Lt. Franks vividly remembers the events of that night. A Vietnam combat veteran, Franks said that the battles fought by the police on April 30 and the days that followed were even more difficult in some respects. "During the riots we were on our own soil, fighting our own citizens," he explained. "It was a very uncomfortable situation."

In addition to developing a plan of action, Lt. Franks had ordered that all police informants be contacted and asked to supply any information relating to the protestors and any activities they were planning. By early evening the intelligence was coming in and the news wasn't good: Gangs that were usually at war with each other had temporarily put their differences aside. They were now united against the police.

By 6:30, gang members were on the streets in force. There were both locals and out-of-towners, primarily from Los Angeles. One group of between 200 and 300 was assembling at Doolittle Park near H Street and Lake Mead. These gangsters had big plans for that night: They were going to march downtown to Fremont Street, Las Vegas' venerable Glitter Gulch. Once they reached their target, the casinos would be looted and at least one of them set afire. Clearly, that couldn't be allowed to happen.

A short time later word came in that the mob at Doolittle Park was on the move on Bonanza, heading downtown. Lt. Franks ordered Sgt. Rory Tuggle to take his squad of 20 officers and establish a skirmish line at a railroad trestle underpass at the intersection of Bonanza and Main. "I told him: There will be no

retreat. Nobody gets by you; they've got to be stopped here."

Sergeant Tuggle assembled his forces and reiterated his orders. "There was no doubt in my mind as to the importance of that assignment," Tuggle recalls. "There was no time for a plan, no briefing or tactical evaluation. The simple truth was, if they got by us, there was nothing between them and downtown."

In riot helmets and with batons at the ready, the cops faced the angry crowd emerging from the underpass. As the rioters met the skirmish line, hand-to-hand combat broke out. For the next several minutes a number of small, sometimes individual, battles were fought, all of them extremely violent. Officers in pairs or alone were attacked by large numbers of assail-

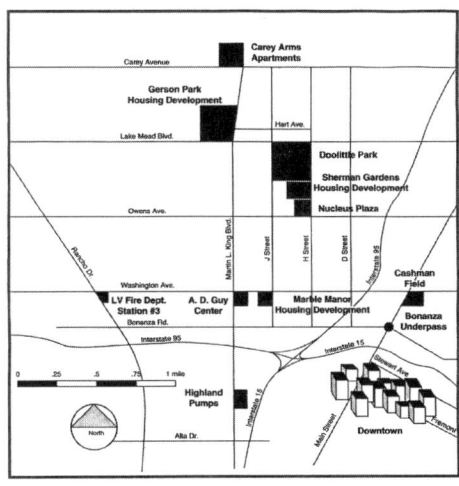

Area of Civil Unrest

ants using fists, feet, clubs, bottles, and rocks against them. They were in fact fighting for their very lives. Although several officers suffered minor injuries, the skirmish line held and the crowd was driven back west on Bonanza.

The incident developed so quickly it hadn't been possible to block traffic on Bonanza, and several unsuspecting motorists became trapped in the underpass. As the rioters retreated they attacked these vehicles with a fury. Windows were broken out and vehicle occupants were punched and kicked.

As the mob began to clear the east side of the underpass, Sgt. Tuggle and Officer Andrew "Andy" Ramos moved forward to assess the situation. They found a white male laying face down in the eastbound driving lane of Bonanza, being kicked and beaten by a group of black males. As the officers approached, the crowd scattered. The victim wasn't moving and was bleeding profusely from the head. The two cops decided to stop their advance and stay with the downed man until an ambulance arrived to remove him. As they crouched next to the victim, a mass of people and pickup trucks with up to 15 male and female occupants came past them, heading westbound. Rocks and bottles were flying at the cops. An empty 40-ounce beer bottle struck Officer Ramos in the helmet, knocking him to the ground. As the pickups went past, Sgt. Tuggle saw occupants in the beds brandishing pistols and firing at them. Bullets whizzed by him, hitting the pavement and ricocheting, sometimes striking the vehicles still stranded in the area. Returning fire was not possible due to the size of the crowd.

Officers were ordered to pursue the fleeing troublemakers and break them into smaller, more manageable units. As the foot pursuit continued, the sound of gunshots increased. One round intended for a cop missed its target and struck a civilian female in the thigh. SWAT and Special Enforcement Detail (SED) personnel were sent into the crowd to provide protection for the victim until an ambulance could extract her.

White People in Jeopardy

Not all of the people in the vicinity of Bonanza and Main were police, protestors, or unwary civilians. The news media had reporters working the streets, too. *Las Vegas Sun* reporter David Clayton was one of them. This account of his experience appeared in the May 1, 1992, edition of the *Sun*:

"'We are being shelled! Attacked!' is all I can remember shouting into my bloodied radio moments after we turned from Main Street onto Bonanza Road.

Ironically, I had just radioed my editor that the marchers were peaceable. 'They're just walking in the direction of downtown, not causing any trouble,' I had reported. To photographer R. Marsh Starks, who was driving, I had speculated about what to expect. A demonstration. Maybe downtown. In a flash it got vicious. A group of young men—perhaps as many as fifty—broke toward our car. One young man in the lead arched back like a baseball pitcher and fired a beer bottle. My sight perception slowed, as if I were in a slow-motion nightmare. I watched the bottle's end-over-end revolutions as it came toward our windshield. The impact shattered the glass as well as my dream state. Starks looked for an escape in traffic. There was none. Astonished, angry, scared, trapped in the car, I screamed into the radio, but could really do nothing but watch and try to shield my head with my arms. There was no helping each other or defending ourselves. A man smashed something—maybe a two-by-four—across our windshield, sending glass flying all over us. Another man approached Marsh's window with a jagged piece of concrete the size of a bowling ball. Standing an inch away he shoved it through the window. On my side, I ducked and covered when a man ran up with what looked like a cinder block. He shoved it through

the window. Marsh took one look at the blood from a deep gash in my neck and lurched his beloved 1969 Mercury out over the center lane. Panicked motorists sideswiped us and we sideswiped them as we whirled west on Bonanza, taking hits from dozens of bottles and rocks as we went. With the left front wheel stripped of its tire, we were forced to abandon the car a few blocks up the road. Marsh's wild drive may very well have saved our lives."

The melee at Bonanza and Main was only the opening round, however. At J Street and McWilliams, another crowd attacked a city mass-transit bus when one of the mob shouted: "White man driving the bus! White man driving the bus!" This observant gangster then opened hostilities by hurling a bottle at the bus. The rest of the crowd joined in, throwing more bottles and rocks. Officers responded to disperse the crowd and rescue the driver.

A Special Enforcement Detail vehicle was struck by gunfire at D Street and Bonanza. As the mob dispersed into the Westside, an LVMPD helicopter reported their movements to ground units who tried to pursue. However, these smaller groups filtered into several housing developments, particularly in the area of McWilliams and N streets.

Reinforcements Arrive

It was now 8 p.m. and dark; there were still not enough personnel available to safely enter the apartment complexes and take control of the situation. The pursuing officers left the area and staged at D Street and Bonanza and at McWilliams and Martin Luther King Boulevard to reorganize and get fresh instructions from the command post.

As these events unfolded, additional personnel from other commands and off-duty status continued to be called in to assist Lt. Franks and his men. In addition to beefing up his forces, Franks had begun the process of sealing off Westside in order to confine the rioters to the smallest area possible. Traffic officers were assigned to key intersections on Bonanza, which became the first secure line. At 8:30, Nevada Highway Patrol was contacted and asked to shut down the freeway ramps leading into the affected area, thereby keeping innocent motorists from wandering into the volatile neighborhoods.

In an effort to curtail the growing use of Molotov cocktails by the mobs, Franks took another prudent action, directing that gas stations only make gasoline sales where the fuel was pumped directly into the vehicle's tank; no containers would be filled.

Bottles, Bricks, and Bullets

During this time, the calls for service coming into the Communications Center had increased by fourfold, with many of them turning out to be false. With the need to efficiently utilize available manpower, Priority Zero call taking was implemented citywide. This meant that the police would only respond to crimes in progress or situations that were life threatening.

On top of that, intelligence was developed causing even more concern about dispatching units: The bad guys planned to call for a police response in order to lure offices into ambushes, where they could be picked off by snipers.

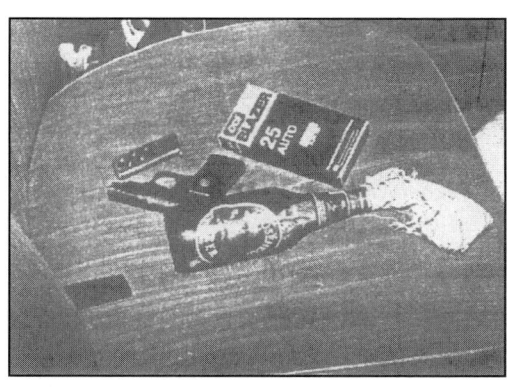

Molotov cocktail

112

The chaos continued and at 8:30 the North Las Vegas Police Department requested Metro's assistance at D Street and Lake Mead Boulevard. A bottle- and brick-throwing crowd was overrunning their officers and gunfire was increasing.

Sergeants Rory Tuggle and Edward Kravetz—fresh from the standoff at Bonanza and Main—and their squads responded to the request for help. Upon their arrival they were met with a hail of rocks, bottles, and bullets. Individuals were observed firing at the police from behind parked cars and the walls of buildings. The tremendous volume of projectiles aimed at them forced personnel from both departments to retreat.

As the withdrawal was taking place, Tuggle and Kravetz received word that units of the Las Vegas Fire Department were under attack while trying to put out a vehicle fire at Martin Luther King and Lake Mead. They headed for that location.

Upon their arrival they found a Volkswagen in the middle of the street completely burned out. It was learned that the driver of that vehicle had been trapped and beaten by a roving group of rioters. Other police units had responded, dispersed the crowd, and extricated the victim. As soon as the cops cleared the scene, the mob returned and torched the car. Although taking gunfire, the responding firemen were able to extinguish the blaze before being driven off. The fire engine sustained a number of bullet holes, but there were no casualties.

Westside in Flames

While still assessing that situation, Sgt. Tuggle and his men were ordered to respond to a report of looting at a shopping center at Martin Luther King and Washington. Upon their arrival they found the windows of several businesses had been shattered and a 7-Eleven store had been looted of its merchandise and cash registers.

Meanwhile, Sgt. Kravetz and his troops went to the Nucleus Shopping Center at H and Owens to regroup. They were greeted by a barrage of rocks, bottles, and hundreds of rounds of gunfire. Two confidential informants who were a part of this particular group of troublemakers later told police that the goal of one of the shooters was to blow the helmets off the heads of the officers. During subsequent conversations, the gang mentioned the names of specific Metro and North Las Vegas cops who were targeted for assassination.

Kravetz and his people initially took cover underneath and behind their vehicles, then withdrew to the field command post at Rancho and Washington.

North Las Vegas again called, requesting assistance in dealing with a group of approximately 300 individuals. Sgt. Tuggle and his squad responded, but were again driven back by the heavy fire. The command post informed North Las Vegas that they would no longer be able to respond to calls for assistance due to a lack of manpower and an increase in their own incidents.

Meanwhile, the rioters turned their attention to the Nucleus Shopping Center itself. Molotov cocktails were thrown onto the roof of the Big 8 Market, the same location of the attacks on the delivery truck driver and three workmen several hours earlier.

The Las Vegas Fire Department responded to fight the ensuing fire. Gunfire forced the firemen to take cover under their vehicles, which sustained numerous bullet holes. It was a very frightening experience for the firemen and a situation for which they were not trained.

Tom Grayson, acting fire department captain, described seeing gunmen firing from the midst of groups of children, knowing that any police in the area would be unable to return fire. This became a common practice for the gangsters throughout the riots. It was a tactic that Lt. Franks later called "acts of extreme cowardice."

After a short time the firemen withdrew, leaving several hoses and other equipment behind and the fire spreading. They wouldn't be able to return until a police escort was provided.

As the firemen left, a crowd of individuals stormed the Big 8 Market and began looting and setting more fires. One of these people was observed leaving the store with rolled coins and boxes of quarters. "Man, it's upstairs; the money is upstairs!" he was heard to shout to the other looters.

The mob was able to get away from the burning building with merchandise and money, all except one. According to witness statements taken later, the looters were forced out of the building by the rapidly expanding fire. While milling around outside they heard someone pounding on the back door from the inside. They attempted to break the door down, but were unsuccessful. The burned remains of the unlucky burglar were found the next day.

At the same time, additional fires were started at an AM/PM Market directly east of the shopping center and at an office complex just south of it. With the area still unsecured, the fire department was forced to hold their response, pending the arrival of the requested police escort.

One of the people involved in that escort was Sgt. Dennis Larsen. Now Lt. Larsen, he remembers that night clearly. "With the electricity out, the only light was from the shopping center buildings burning. It was very eerie; I kept thinking that this was what a combat zone in Beirut would be like," he says.

Larsen was part of a group of 14 officers and two K-9s. Their first assignment upon arrival was to remove what was thought to be a group of looters raiding the shops and offices. It turned out that the "looters" were actually business owners and some firemen who had returned and were assessing the situation.

The area of the parking lot in which the cops were staging was swept with gunfire, bullets whining through the air like swarms of angry bees. Due to dense smoke and other conditions, the police were not able to return fire.

In Larsen's opinion: "The motive of the rioters had nothing to do with showing support for Rodney King. They were there to commit violence."

At 9:30 the fire department made another effort to combat the blaze that now engulfed half the shopping center and the nearby buildings. This attempt ended quickly as well, when gunfire forced another retreat.

Police Under Direct Attack

As if the police and firemen didn't already have a full plate, word was received that the unmanned Metro substation on Silverman Avenue was ablaze. Responding officers found the building had been looted and police equipment was strewn about outside.

While waiting for the fire department to arrive, officers took sporadic sniper fire, but held their ground. Firemen were able to extinguish the flames before they spread to apartment buildings located close by.

As that battle was being fought, word was received that another substation, located at the Gerson Park Housing Development, was burning. Fifteen officers under the direction of Sgt. Mike McClary responded to the scene. Upon their arrival they found a situation similar to the one on Silverman Avenue. While attempting to secure a perimeter to admit the fire department, the cops came under heavy gunfire, pinning them down. Reinforcements arrived and the officers battled the blaze with extinguishers from their vehicles and managed to put out the fire themselves. As the police exited the area, they took additional gunfire.

Three officers who were attempting to get to the Gerson Park incident never made it. Ralph

Ray, Randy Mayberry, and Chris Embree were in a vehicle, with Ray driving. As they entered the intersection of Martin Luther King and Lake Mead, they encountered two groups totaling approximately 300 people on opposite sides of the street. Their arrival was met with the customary bottle and rock throwing, followed by the distinct sound of four gunshots; the driver's window shattered, with broken glass showering the occupants. Several of these fragments struck Officer Mayberry's eyes.

The driver, Officer Ray, immediately yelled out: "I've been shot! I've been shot!" as a torrent of blood spurted out of his left arm. Ray maintained control of the vehicle while Mayberry radioed a report and tried to locate a secure area to pull over and apply first aid. Unfortunately, safe areas were few and far between.

After passing through several more hostile crowds, the three cops finally found an area of relative calm at Carey and Donna streets. Officer Ray was placed in the back seat where Mayberry applied a piece of cloth from a torn shirt to the wound in an effort to stem the bleeding. While that was going on, Officer Embree jumped into the driver's seat and raced for North Las Vegas Hospital.

Officer Ray was admitted in a state of shock from blood loss. Embree and Mayberry were treated and later returned to duty, providing escort for ambulances responding inside the combat zone.

While all this was going on, the Super 6 Market at Martin Luther King and Lake Mead was looted and put to the torch. However, the area could not be secured sufficiently for a fire department response.

Rookies Hold the Line

That night, Sgt. Steve Custer, a 19-year veteran, was in charge of two squads totaling 16 officers. Most of them were fairly new with Metro, many with about a year on the job.

Ten years after the riots, Custer recalled what occurred. "Those rookie rapidly became seasoned officers," he says of their transformation under fire. "The training and professionalism of the frontline supervisors and the quality of the officers they commanded saved the day."

Custer remembers responding to the Nucleus Shopping Center to assist the fire department after the confrontation at Bonanza and Main. "Heavy fire drove both us and the firemen to take cover in and under the fire trucks. You could hear the rounds pinging off those vehicles," he says.

He agrees with other witnesses that the attacking gunmen surrounded themselves with children to assure they wouldn't receive return fire.

One of the officers under Custer's command was Todd Fasulo. Now a sergeant with the K-9 Detail, he says, "I was supposed to be at my best friend's wedding at five that afternoon. Of course, I never made it."

Fasulo had finished his Field Training five months earlier and was still learning the ropes. He believes that in addition to the training provided by Metro, his prior military experience helped him deal with the events of April 30.

"My first assignment that night was to assist the fire department at a car fire at Bonanza and Martin Luther King. There was a hostile crowd of about two hundred on the scene and they were throwing rocks and bottles mixed with gunfire," he recalls.

LVMPD officers being briefed at the staging area.

In Fasulo's mind, outstanding frontline supervision and the decision to take the offensive against the rioters made the difference between success and failure.

Before the night was over, Todd Fasulo became one of the seasoned veterans Sgt. Custer was so proud of.

Police Maintain Presence

As the night wore on and the violence mounted, the command post was a hive of activity. Additional personnel continued to be mobilized and meetings were held between appropriate department leaders, who discussed whether to adhere to earlier strategies or implement new ideas.

There were three schools of thought on how to proceed: contain the rioters in the smallest possible area; avoid additional casualties and withdraw all personnel from the hot spots until the danger subsided on its own; or stay on the offensive and deal with the criminals who were causing the violence.

Lieutenant Franks was still in favor of the latter strategy. Having watched the problems in Los Angeles on television the previous night, he saw the devastation that occurred when the cops retreated from an area. He felt it was the moral, professional, and ethical duty of the police to stay in the area and confront the situation, not abandon the innocent citizens to the mercy of the rabble. Franks proposed that a curfew be imposed. He would then split the area into five sectors and drive a wedge into any large crowds of violators. Once dispersed into smaller groups, they would be arrested.

After much debate, the Lieutenant's plan was approved. He would be ready to take the initiative as soon as the necessary personnel and equipment could be deployed.

Las Vegas Mayor Jan Jones arrived at the command post at 9:30. Briefed on what had transpired so far and the plan suggested by Lt. Franks, she consulted the City Attorney, then agreed to a curfew beginning at 10:30 and lasting through dawn until further notice. At 10 p.m. the mayor issued a press release announcing the curfew.

An hour later the cops were staging in the parking lot next to the K-Mart at Rancho Road and Washington Avenue. The officers assembled for deployment included 100 new arrivals and 60 who had already been in combat for more than 10 hours. The latter had been given a chance to eat and rest. The group included SWAT, SED, and K-9 units, as well as several correctional officers and the jail bus. After a briefing, the cops left the staging area; the effort to take back Westside was about to begin.

Some officers were sent to specific traffic-control points along Bonanza, Rancho, Lake Mead, Commerce, and Main. Their orders were to stop all traffic attempting to enter or leave the areas of containment.

Those attempting to enter could proceed only if they had a residence address inside the containment zones, but not in a section that was still experiencing gunfire. Motorists with addresses outside the trouble spots were turned away. Individuals attempting to leave were stopped and questioned. If it didn't appear they would pose a problem elsewhere, they were permitted to go on their way. If an individual or group seemed likely to cause trouble later on, they were identified, questioned, and monitored as they left.

After the outer perimeter was established, other officers were assigned to the five sectors designated by Lt. Franks. Additional perimeters were set up around each sector and officers announced the curfew. If a crowd didn't comply, officers moved into the group and separated the violators into smaller and more manageable numbers, then the arrests began.

Mass Arrests Begin

As these assignments were being carried out, another operation was taking place at H Street and Owens Avenue, the location of the Nucleus Shopping Center. Westside couldn't be brought under control if the gangs were allowed to remain in charge in this key area.

Sergeants Rory Tuggle, John Russo, Gary Schofield, and Dennis Larsen and 80 officers were assigned. They rode four officers to a vehicle and the jail bus accompanied their caravan.

Upon their arrival the force split into four squads, two of which went directly into the Nucleus Shopping Center. A third entered the Sherman Gardens Apartments located on J Street, just west of the shopping center. The fourth squad proceeded to the Sherman Gardens Housing Development, slightly to the north. K-9 were deployed with these squads.

For the next hour, they moved through the shopping center and the two housing areas, encountering small groups of troublemakers, snipers, and heavy gunfire. As individuals were taken into custody, they were placed in flex cuffs and escorted to the jail bus.

As the bus filled, one of the prisoners who had somehow gotten aboard with a concealed box cutter freed himself and cut the cuffs off several other arrestees. They trashed the inside of the vehicle and kicked out windows. Officers had to wade in with mace to regain control of the bus. During this incident one prisoner sustained injuries requiring hospitalization, another escaped and was recaptured, and a corrections officer suffered a fractured leg.

A total of 80 adults and eight juveniles were arrested during the various operations. In addition to the jail bus, a paddy wagon was put into service to move the arrestees. Some officers transported their own prisoners.

Throughout the night citizens living in the combat areas called for help in medical-related emergencies. Many of these involved people who couldn't use their oxygen equipment due to power outages and depletion of their batteries. After these calls were verified as legitimate, an ambulance was dispatched, accompanied by multiple police vehicles, each containing four officers.

Police Take Control

By 3 the next morning the police had gained the upper hand. A firm outer perimeter was in place and four of the five sectors were under control; the fire department was again battling the many fires. More manpower arrived through the night, relieving the exhausted officers who had been on the front lines since the previous afternoon. As the sun rose on the morning of May 1, a new and larger command post was ready for operation at Cashman Field. Governor Bob Miller approved a request for deployment of a National Guard military police unit; the 100 Guardsmen would be deployed to the new command post by that evening. The FBI contributed a Vietnam-era V100 Armored Personnel Carrier that was delivered to the command post. Additional personnel were continuing to arrive and Westside was relatively quiet. As the day progressed and the area remained calm, the perimeter was removed.

Fright Night was over, but Fright Night II was still to come.

The Opposing Sides Regroup

Over the next several days, elected officials, police managers, leaders of the black community, and representatives of the various gangs met to try and identify the underlying problems that had caused the violence of April 30.

Separately, the cops were analyzing their own performance and deciding on strategies to help return Westside to normalcy. They decided to establish face-to-face communications with the citizens, build trust, gather information, support enforcement actions, and facilitate community-based solutions to problems.

Officers were directed to walk foot patrol and interact with the residents. They were urged to discuss what had occurred and elicit suggestions for the future. They were further instructed to contact gang leaders and let them know that criminal activity would not be tolerated and that the police would not back away from violence.

However, in case these outreach efforts were unsuccessful, non-lethal projectiles were ordered as an extra option in dealing with any future mob violence.

With the cops back in the neighborhoods, fresh intelligence began to come in, some of it alarming. During the ensuing week it was learned that the Blood and Crip gangs had declared a long-term truce. The gangsters said they had merged on the night of April 30 and were now calling themselves the Black Brotherhood. They declared that the police were now the enemy and vowed that Westside would never be the same.

Confidential informants further maintained that local gangs were actively encouraging their associates from Los Angeles to come to Las Vegas to teach them the riot techniques they'd used so successfully in Los Angeles. In addition, the Las Vegans were interested in instruction on the proper way to commit commercial burglaries and robberies. The locals had targeted a pawnshop and a gun store they thought would yield large supplies of weapons and ammo; they wanted to make sure they did the jobs right.

Another plan allegedly being discussed was for some Westside gang members to start a commotion large enough to require a major police response, drawing officers from other areas into Westside to assist. This disturbance would only be a diversion, however. While the cops were occupied, pre-positioned gang members would roam throughout Clark County, looting businesses and residences.

The gangs planned to continue the civil disobedience for as long as they could maintain sufficient forces to keep the movement active. The idea of luring officers into an ambush with bogus calls for assistance was also still under consideration. Another scheme called for officers to be set up by having a vehicle commit a traffic infraction within view of a patrol car. While the officers were busy with the traffic stop, a second car full of gang members would drive by and shoot at the otherwise occupied officers.

Several of these false calls did in fact come in when the gangsters gathered. One claimed that several black males at a gang gathering were sexually assaulting a white girl. The call could not be confirmed, so officers were not sent into the crowd, but monitored the gathering instead. It was later learned that this incident was one of the ambush attempts and that no rape had occurred.

The LVMPD command staff directed officers to allow these gang gatherings to continue unless overt criminal activity was observed. Their reasoning was that the truce between the gangs could actually have a positive effect on the crime rate in Westside. The number of drive-by shootings and other acts of violence between the gangs that frequently resulted in injury or death to innocent people had dropped off sharply, which was good. The downside, of course, was that all of their violence was now directed at the police.

A Second Round of Violence

Thursday, May 8, marked the approach of the second weekend following Fright Night. Few positive results from the continuing meetings between government and community leaders were in evidence that day, as the gang gatherings became larger and more violent. Both the North Las Vegas Police Department and Metro experienced increased calls relating to civil disobedience.

Late that evening a crowd of 200 attacked security guards at the Carey Arms Apartment Complex in NLVPD territory with bottles and rocks. After firing several warning shots into the air, the guards were escorted out of the area by NLVPD officers.

An equal number of rowdies gathered at Gerson Park housing development in Westside. A report was received that nearly every gang in Las Vegas was represented in this crowd. The usual rock and bottle throwing occurred, accompanied by gunfire. In anticipation of escalating aggression, a command post was established nearby and additional personnel were assembled. However, the crowd dispersed around 3:30 the next morning without any major incidents.

Showdown

The night of Friday, May 9, brought similar problems at Gerson Park, but on a larger scale. A crowd estimated at 300 was involved and intelligence had been received that an ambush was planned.

Around midnight a Metro unit attempted to stop a vehicle for a traffic violation near Gerson Park. The vehicle's operator refused to comply and drove into the apartment complex. Fearing an ambush, officers decided not to pursue the car into the ever-increasing crowd.

However, Lt. Franks was contacted at home and briefed on the situation. A patrol car containing Sgts. Steve Custer, Curtis Williams, and John Russo picked up the Lieutenant, then drove him to Gerson Park Development for a first-hand analysis of the conditions. These four men decided to enter the complex and talk to members of the crowd to learn their intent and possibly de-escalate the hostility.

As their car entered the area and approached the mob, four vehicles pulled in behind them, blocking any retreat; the only other way out required passing through the crowd to the other side of the complex.

As they navigated through the sea of bodies, rioters attempted to pull Custer and Russo from the car through the open windows. A barrage of rocks, bottles, and gunshots followed. The crowd eventually opened up and the officers escaped, driving over lawns and curbs. While they were driving away the shots continued, muzzle flashes lighting the night.

Just as they outdistanced the gunmen, the cops encountered a vehicle loaded with known gang members. A pedestrian yelled that

Officers taking cover at Marting Luther King and Owens Avenue

shots had been fired at him from that car. During the high-speed chase, other units stopped the subject vehicle and the suspects were arrested.

Franks decided to return to Gerson Park to check for anyone injured during the gunfire and to look for any evidence that could be used for possible criminal prosecution. Franks and the three sergeants, accompanied by five two-officer units, parked on Carver Street and walked into the complex. Encountering heavy sniper fire, the cops took cover behind the buildings. Criminalistics personnel later recovered 16 9mm casings in the area from which the shots originated.

As the officers were trying to pinpoint the origin of the firing, four individuals were observed approaching their positions. The four split into two pairs and continued forward in crouched positions between the buildings. Russo and Custer, who had separated from Franks and Williams, noted two subjects who appeared to be carrying weapons and heading for the Lieutenant's position. As the subjects approached, Lt. Franks happened to round the corner of the building, facing the two individuals head-on. One had a rifle and the other a shotgun. Franks, in civilian clothes, drew his gun, identified himself, and ordered the weapons dropped. At that moment another subject emerged from the door to one of the apartments. The Lieutenant turned his attention to the potential new threat and ordered him to the ground. He then heard a gunshot go off nearby. He swung around to find the man with the rifle pointing the weapon at him. He again ordered the two men to put down their weapons. When they refused, he fired one shot at them. The pair, still armed, turned and ran. Franks gave chase and fired two more rounds, striking the man with the rifle, who dropped to the ground.

This suspect, a self-acknowledged gang member, sustained a wound to his upper right arm. Found next to him was a loaded rifle, a 30-round magazine, and two pieces of rock cocaine. He was transported to University Medical Center Hospital for treatment and eventually lost his arm. He was subsequently charged and convicted for his attack on Lt. Franks and possessing the cocaine and was sentenced to three five-year prison terms.

A seven-member Use of Force Board later investigated this incident and found that the use of force by Lt. Franks was fully justified.

The second suspect got away, but a Mossberg 12-gauge shotgun with pistol grips and loaded with six shells was found nearby.

By 3 a.m. a force of 80 officers and SWAT personnel had dispersed the crowd and Gerson Park quieted down.

Another Bad Night

Saturday, May 10, progressed without serious incident during the morning and early afternoon. But tensions were especially high due to the previous night's shooting. Sergeant Bob Gronauer, with many years working Westside, entered the Gerson Park Complex on foot around 2 p.m. and struck up a conversation with a group of Crips and Bloods with whom he was familiar. They told him that both sides bore responsibility for the shooting: the gang members for firing first and the police for driving into the complex in a four-man unit with the back doors open, as though they were looking for trouble. They also told him that they planned to hold a football game that evening, but promised there would be no trouble. The football game was later cancelled in favor of a baseball game at the A.D. Guy Center at Washington and Martin Luther King.

By 6 that evening the planned baseball game, which never occurred, turned into a party of about 300, mainly in the parking lot of the Guy Center, but also spilling into the street. The crowd was large and loud, with a lot of beer being consumed. Officers entered the throng and spoke with the leaders. It was agreed that the gathering could continue as long as there was no violence or overt criminal activity.

As darkness fell, the baseball field and parking lot lights were turned on. This action served both the crowd (convenience) and the cops (more efficient surveillance). In the event things got out of control, a command post was established nearby and personnel, including SWAT and the FBI's armored personnel carrier, were staged there. A supply of the non-lethal projectiles ordered after April 30 was now available.

By 10 p.m. the composition of the gathering had changed for the worse. Most of the children and older adults had left. The people remaining were much more intoxicated and vocal. However, since there was no violence or criminal activity evident, the police honored their agreement and let the gathering continue. The SED units maintained their surveillance from a distance.

At 10:30 a fight broke out in the Guy Center parking lot between two of the attendees. One of the participants pulled a gun from his waistband and fired several shots into the air. Angered by this incident, the crowd forced the gunman to leave. As he drove away, monitoring SED officers alerted patrol units and the suspect was apprehended.

After the troublemaker had been ejected, the crowd, now numbering approximately 200, moved across the street from the Guy Center and into the Marble Manor Housing Development. Concerned about this movement, Sgt. Rory Tuggle responded from the command post and spoke with several gang leaders. He was assured that this was a peaceful gathering and that the man with the gun was uninvited and not representative of the rest of the group.

Satisfied, Tuggle said the assembly could continue as long as there were no problems. He ordered that the mess being created by the crowd be cleaned up. The gang leaders organized a crew and the empty bottles, cans, and other debris were gathered and put in dumpsters. Tuggle returned to the staging area at the command post.

At around 11 p.m., the police received a report of looting at a 7-Eleven store just north of the Guy Center. Responding officers found that some of the store's windows had been broken out, but the offenders had already left the area.

At 11:30, an SED officer observed a subject known to him by name throw a brick through one of the remaining windows of the same 7-Eleven store, then retreat back into the crowd at Marble Manor. Officers were dispatched to arrest this individual.

Tuggle approached the crowd and asked to speak with the gang leaders who had been cooperative earlier; he was told they had all left. Tuggle announced that he didn't want to end the gathering, but a criminal act had occurred and the suspect had to be arrested.

Upon that news, the crowd began to circle the cops, yelling epithets and threats. Since the identity of the suspect was known and he could be arrested another time, the officers retreated from the increasingly hostile mob. As the cops neared their vehicles, the rock and bottle throwing began. Tuggle declared that the gathering had now become unlawful and had to disperse. About half of the mob complied, but a hard core of about 100 defiant people remained.

Reinforcements were sent to the scene and a skirmish line of 30 officers was formed to advance on the group. The majority of the crowd retreated farther into the Marble Manor Complex as the police moved forward; those who didn't were taken into custody by arrest teams.

As the skirmish line reached Morgan Street, the police were bombarded by thrown projectiles and gunfire. With the officers now facing high risk of injury or death, the skirmish line was disbanded and a new tactic employed.

The Armored Personnel Carrier was brought in from the staging area and the non-lethal munitions were put into play. The APC advanced into the combat zone, an FBI agent driving. Three SWAT officers armed with gas guns that could fire the non-lethal baton rounds were also in the vehicle; three more walked behind the unit, armed with shotguns that could fire non-lethal stinger ammo.

As the cops moved into the housing complex, they took heavy gunfire, estimated at 50 rounds. Non-lethal fire was returned, striking many of the suspects. This tactic caused the crowd to disperse. The action was discontinued when police helicopter reported that no remaining groups of violators were visible in the complex.

By 1 a.m. the area was secured. Peace and quiet returned to Westside, for the time being.

Fright Night II

City Councilman Frank Hawkins sponsored a gathering, called "Community Coming Together Picnic," on Friday, May 16, at Doolittle Park, located at Lake Mead Boulevard and J Street. The event was heavily advertised through flyers and a local radio station. Councilman Hawkins met with LVMPD of-

Armored Personnel Carrier

ficials, including Lt. Franks, and assured them the picnic would be peaceful and that he would be in attendance.

The picnic began at 1 that afternoon and quickly grew to more than 1,000 people. The size of the crowd dictated that a command post be established at the Northwest Area Command Station. The necessary resources to deal with any potential problems were staged at Cashman Field. The gathering began much as Councilman Hawkins had promised: well attended and peaceful. Families and children were plentiful and the mood was festive.

By late afternoon, however, that atmosphere was changing. The command post received word that the crowd at Doolittle Park was planning to march downtown. The motives were conflicting, ranging from a peaceful rally at City Hall to looting and vandalism on Fremont Street. This latter scenario was similar to the intent of the rioters on April 30. With these ominous rumblings, Fright Night II began.

By 6 p.m., 56 officers had assembled at Cashman Field. They were briefed, then sent to Main Street Station, the first casino the marchers would encounter. At 7 p.m., an additional 45 officers were dispatched to City Hall. By 9 p.m. the command post was satisfied that the chances of an assault on downtown had diminished sufficiently to recall these officers to a new staging area at the Costco store on Martin Luther King Boulevard; SWAT personnel and two Peacekeeper APCs were also at this location.

By that time, the mood of the crowd at Doolittle Park was menacing. As with other gatherings, after the children and older adults had gone home, only the more hostile individuals remained.

Three officers were ordered to get closer to the picnickers, monitor them, and videotape any illegal activity. Sergeant Gronauer and detectives Ed Landino and Gene Marshall drove to the vicinity. Unseen in the darkness, they walked into a desert area within several feet of the crowd now estimated at 300, mostly gang members, teenagers, and young adults.

As the three cops watched, the crowd suddenly spilled out onto Lake Mead and H Street. Fights broke out between some of the gang members; one person had to be transported to the hospital after being assaulted by several individuals. The injured man, interviewed by police at the hospital, said the gang truce was breaking down and that he had observed a large number of weapons in the crowd still at Doolittle Park.

In the meantime, cars with

rioters riding on roofs, hoods, and trunks drove through the jammed intersection of Lake Mead and H Street and the surrounding area, firing weapons as they went. At one point two of these vehicles collided, sending one of the hood riders flying to the pavement. After landing, he was run over by several other vehicles. He was transported to the hospital, but died of his injuries a week later.

At 10:30, several cars with white occupants inadvertently entered the mob-controlled area on Lake Mead. One vehicle, driven by an off-duty security guard, was attacked; the man was beaten, hit in the head with a 40-ounce beer bottle, and robbed. All the car windows were smashed.

Soon after, a car occupied by four white teenagers entered the same vicinity. Their vehicle was surrounded and an assault ensued. One of the teenagers was hit in the head with another 40-ounce bottle, causing him to temporarily lose his vision.

At 11 p.m. the command post ordered the three observers to withdraw. The situation was deteriorating and heading toward riot conditions. The time for action had arrived.

At 11:15, a dispersal order was issued. The two APCs, each manned by a driver and six SWAT officers, were put into motion to deliver the message to the crowd, now estimated at 350. The vehicles drove northbound on Martin Luther King, then turned on Lake Mead facing east. From that position the announcement was made by loudspeaker that the gathering was an unlawful assembly and had 10 minutes to disperse.

That statement drew a torrent of rocks and bottles and a barrage of gunfire. The APCs withdrew to the west to wait out the 10-minute ultimatum. When they returned, it would be to fire tear gas into any remnants of the mob that remained. The plan called for the tear gas to force the gangsters to retreat into the waiting arms of 80 officers staged at the intersection of Carey and Revere. The jail bus and a contingent of correction officers were also at that location.

At midnight the APCs again advanced and deployed four tear-gas grenades into the crowd. As the mob moved eastbound, the force at Cary and Revere advanced. As the two groups met, the mob unleashed a salvo of rocks, bottles, and gunfire. An object crashed through the windshield of one of the police vehicles, completely shattering it. The crowd, now numbering 400, then headed north and west to the Carey Arms Apartment Complex in North Las Vegas.

At 12:35 a.m. the NLVPD requested Metro's assistance in

dealing with the mob. The request was approved at 12:45 and the two Peacekeeper APCs, now joined by the FBI's V100 vehicle and manned by SWAT personnel, entered the complex. All other officers were ordered to stay out of the area due to the exceptionally heavy gunfire.

As these armored units advanced, they broadcast a dispersal order. But all hell broke loose. In what one SWAT sergeant described as "the worst encounter yet," hundreds of rounds were fired at them from rooftops and ground level. Reportedly, mob members fired twice on the police with fully automatic weapons.

SWAT officers responded with more than 200 rounds of non-lethal ammunition, several tear gas canisters, and sound-and-flash distraction devices. The crowd in the Carey Arms Complex was disbanded by 1:15 and the area declared secure. Metro personnel withdrew to their own territory to rest and regroup. Their night's work, however, was not quite over.

At around 1:30, a radio call announced that businesses at the intersection of Ernest May and Rancho were being looted. The first two officers to arrive found a group of about 100 people exiting the Footlocker and Kinney Shoes stores, carrying armloads of good-

ies. As the cops drove closer to the crowd, the looters began to run away. One of the more clumsy thieves tripped and fell into the patrol car, one of the easier arrests of the night.

The gang from the shoe stores regrouped and joined a couple hundred other gangsters in the parking lot of a nearby sports bar. The police on the scene requested reinforcements. This particular group dispersed on its own and without additional incident, however.

At 2 a.m., reports came in of a large gathering and shots fired at the Gerson Park Housing Development, the scene of many previous problems. The APCs and SWAT officers were dispatched to the complex, again armed with tear gas and non-lethal munitions. A force of 50 officers under the direction of four sergeants was positioned around Gerson Park. They would snare escaping individuals for questioning and make arrests if necessary.

The operation began at 2:30 and lasted an hour; 15 persons were arrested on charges ranging from curfew violation to aiming a deadly weapon. Total arrests that night numbered 32, keeping the jail bus and several paddy wagons busy.

By 6 a.m., Westside had completely quieted down and personnel retired from the area.

New Strategies

Although Fright Night II was over, the events of that night had a profound impact on government officials, community leaders, Westside residents, and the police.

The officials, leaders, and police realized that the attempts to reach out to the gangs and continuing to allow mass assemblies had failed. Regardless of the initial intent, these gatherings had invariably turned to violence; a new strategy had to be implemented.

The citizens of Westside had had enough, too. The vast majority of the residents were hard working and law abiding. Their neighborhoods had been taken over by the gangs. Many of them became victims of crimes and virtually all of them were prisoners who were afraid to leave their homes. They wanted their streets back.

On May 17, Sheriff Moran ordered that all groups of six persons or more who were congregating for unlawful purposes would be immediately dispersed. This policy was reviewed by the Las Vegas City Attorney's Office and found to be constitutional.

In an unprecedented move, the Las Vegas Police Protective Association offered a reward of up to $10,000 for information leading to the arrest and conviction of anyone committing a felony against its members. Union leaders hoped the reward offer would act as a deterrent to the threats and violence being directed against its officers.

The several days after Fright Night II were a time of high tensions between the police and gang members of Westside and North Las Vegas. The days were generally quiet; as darkness fell, however, the gangs gathered, guns were fired, and disturbing intelligence reports were received. One scenario was that a gas truck was going to be stolen and run into the North Las Vegas Police station. Area sporting-goods stores reported that black males were making unusually large purchases of ammunition.

On May 20, a confidential informant provided a chilling insight into what the gangs had in mind. According to the informant, a "gang unification party" was planned for the Guy Center in the near future to solidify the relationship between the gangs and to plan future actions against the police.

The gangsters felt that they had to again defy the cops when their groups were ordered to disperse. To do so, West Coast Bloods were attempting to obtain more guns to arm their own members and those of other gangs as well. They were aware that the police were operating at above-normal staffing levels, but would be unable to maintain those numbers indefinitely. When things returned to normal, the gangs would seek their revenge.

Pursuant to the informant's information, police officials developed an operational plan. It called for pre-positioning officers in the problem housing developments, the immediate dispersal of gang gatherings of six persons or more, and the assignment of SWAT personnel, supported by patrol and SED officers, in response to a refusal to disperse. Specific tactics to be used would be determined by the Field Commander in charge of the operation.

At approximately 9 p.m. on May 25, North Las Vegas requested Metro's assistance with a crowd of around 250 people forming at Valley View Park, located at the intersection of Travis and Gilday. Metro and North Las Vegas SWAT teams in APCs entered the problem area and gave the dispersal order. After the announcement, the crowd hurled bottles and rocks and a bullet struck one APC. The police responded with stun grenades and other non-lethal rounds. In a few minutes the park was cleared and Metro personnel withdrew.

This gathering turned out to be the last that Metro had to deal with. As the weeks passed, normal conditions gradually returned to Westside. Although isolated incidents continued throughout the summer, the organized and violent mass gatherings were over.

The incidents in Las Vegas weren't as severe as those in Los Angeles, but they had resulted in substantial financial loss, property damage, and injury. Incredibly, no one on either side died as a result of gunfire.

In the days and months following the period of civil unrest, the police continued to reach out to the residents of Westside, to become partners with them in policing their community and keeping the streets safe. The lessons learned by Metro between April 30 and May 25 were used to develop plans for dealing with similar situations that may occur in the future.

Hopefully, those plans will never have to be implemented.

6

The Keller and Young Eras

Sheriff Jerry Keller

Introduction

In January 1995, Jerry Keller was sworn in as Clark County Sheriff, replacing John Moran. A lifetime Las Vegan, he graduated from Western High School in 1964 and began his law-enforcement career with the Clark County Sheriff's Department in 1969. After stints in Patrol, Criminalistics, and Internal Affairs, he attained the rank of sergeant in 1975 and made lieutenant in 1983. He served as commander of the SWAT and K-9 units and started the Street Narcotics unit prior to advancing to captain in 1987. Promoted to Deputy Chief of Administrative Services in 1993, he won election as Sheriff in 1994. Keller headed the department for eight years, stepping down at the end of his second term. Most agree

Jerry Keller

that his administration continued the modernization of Metro that John Moran had started.

When Jerry Keller took office in 1995, the population of Metro's jurisdiction was 824,050. He commanded a force of 1,360 police officers and 328 corrections officers. It was not only a large department, it was a busy one, too. During that first year the Communications Center handled 533,830 calls on its 9-1-1 lines; Search and Rescue responded to 103 situations; the Patrol Division was dispatched to 323,077 requests for service; the Detention Center had 46,234 incarcerations; K-9 answered 4,897 calls; Traffic handled 84 fatalities; 13,157 crime scenes were processed; Vice had 512 felony and gross misdemeanor arrests; the SWAT unit executed 458 search warrants, and Special Events coordinated 1,422 events. Metro's total expenses were $148,226,097.

New Programs

In 1996, the department, the population it served, and the number of tourists visiting Las Vegas continued to grow at a phenomenal pace. New programs were implemented that dealt with ways to prevent crime when possible, and more effectively deal with the perpetrators when prevention failed.

One of these initiatives targeted the problem of young girls turning to prostitution on the streets of Las Vegas. Operation STOP (Stop Turning Out Prostitutes) was launched in January 1997 in an effort to reform young prostitutes.

Under this new program, these children—mostly between the ages of 12 and 17—were treated as victims rather than offenders. Those eligible were sent to a shelter and rehabilitative program in Los Angeles called Children of the Night. During the year, 68 young girls were arrested in Las Vegas and 14 were sent to the shelter. Fifty-two adults were arrested on charges related to pimping a child.

Another program targeting prostitution began in January 1997. Implemented by Metro and Municipal Court, the "John" school allowed clients of prostitutes to attend a one-day class to learn the downside of patronizing a prostitute. The class cost the defendant $500 and was in lieu of all other fines and punishment.

In February 1998, the Metro Volunteer Program was instituted. Volunteers were recruited to serve in areas where their expertise or service would benefit the department and community. Candidates went through a thorough background investigation prior to being accepted into the program.

In May 1998, the Domestic Violence Detail was established. Working out of the Detective Bureau, this unit was tasked with conducting vigorous follow-up investigations of cases of domestic violence and related crimes such as battery, stalking, and harassment.

Tourist Protection

Another area that received special attention was tourism. Tens of millions of tourists pass through Las Vegas every year. Many of these visitors come to gamble and party. Most bring ample spending money with them; they're in town looking to have a good time. In that frame of mind, they might not always be as alert as they should be. It stands to reason that oblivious tourists must be ripe for the plucking by muggers, pickpockets, and con artists. Tourists must account for most of the crime victims in Vegas, right?

Wrong.

Lieutenant Larry Spinosa is in charge of Metro's Tourist Safety Unit. Established in May 1996, the unit is composed of two squads, with six detectives assigned to each. Except for homicides and sexual assaults, they're responsible for investigating crimes against tourists that occur in what's called the "tourist corridor." This includes the Strip, downtown, or any establishment with 200 or more rooms and live gaming. The bulk of the incidents investigated by Spinosa's unit are room burglaries, purse snatchings, pocket picking, and theft of credit cards.

According to the Las Vegas Convention and Visitors Authority, 35,849,000 people visited Las Vegas in 2000. In 2001, including the impact of the events of September 11, there were just over 35,000,000 tourists.

Even with all these potential targets, only 4,778 crimes against tourists were reported in 2001. In fact, although the number of tourists has increased nearly every year, reported crimes against them were down by 20% since 1997.

Spinosa is quick to point out that hotel security personnel are an integral part of the efforts to protect tourists. He cites their professionalism and cooperation with his unit as major factors in the successes being enjoyed.

A situation frequently exploited by the criminals is closing thanks to modern technology. In the past, offenders have often had the charges against them dismissed because their victims failed to return to Vegas to testify. However, Lt. Spinosa says a law passed in 2001 has all but eliminated that problem. This statute allows the victim to appear against the defendant during court proceedings via teleconference. No longer having to incur the time and expense of appearing in person to testify has greatly enhanced the odds that these perpetrators will be held accountable for their crimes.

Drive-by

At approximately 1 a.m. on December 28, 1996, six young men were standing in an alley behind

McKellar Circle, near Paradise and Flamingo roads. A pickup truck occupied by two males made its way down the alley toward the men. As it neared them, six rounds were fired out the passenger side window from a handgun. The pickup continued on and left the area. One of the group, 21-year-old Daniel Mendoza, was mortally wounded in the attack.

Unfortunately, this scenario is repeated much too often in cities all across the country. Many times these drive-by shootings involve rival gang members or drug dealers, people out for their idea of revenge, or to eliminate the competition. This case was far from being a routine criminal-on-criminal act of violence, however. The two men in the pickup truck that morning weren't gangbangers. They didn't

Ron Mortensen

have criminal records. On the contrary, they were both off-duty police officers.

Homicide Detective Brent Becker didn't know that when he was first assigned to the case, of course. Witnesses agreed that the passenger was the shooter; he was white and "looked like a cop." Based on his initial investigation, Detective Becker wasn't optimistic about the chances for a quick arrest. Nonetheless, a mere 36 hours after the shooting, the case broke wide open.

"My sergeant called and said there had been a big break in the Mendoza case," Becker recalls. He was told to come into the office and meet two people who had information about the killing. One of the individuals was Mike Brady, a 29-year police veteran. The second person was Brady's son, Christopher, with three years as a Metro officer. The younger Brady told Becker that the pickup truck involved in the incident was his and he'd been behind the wheel at the time. Brady also surrendered the murder weapon. He said the gun belonged to his partner, who'd been in the truck with him and shot Mendoza. He identified his companion as Officer Ron Mortensen.

Brady told Detective Becker that he and Mortensen had been out celebrating Mortensen's birthday on the night of the 27th and into the early morning of the 28th. They had consumed quite a bit of alcohol and were traveling from one bar to another when they decided to take a detour into the McKellar Circle neighborhood, an area with a predominantly Hispanic population. Their intention was to harass any of the local gangsters they found on the streets. When they encountered the group in the alley, Mortensen pulled his gun and opened fire. Brady said that when Mortensen fired his weapon, it came as a complete surprise to him. Unaware that anyone had been hit, he drove to another bar. The pair went in for more drinks, with Mortensen leaving his gun in the truck. Brady said that when he was watching television the next day, he learned of Mendoza's death. He called his father, who arranged for him to turn himself in.

"He asked me what was going to happen to him," Becker said. "I told him he'd probably be charged as an accessory to murder." However, after consultation with the District Attorney's Office, it was decided to treat Brady as a witness and not arrest him at that point.

That evening, Ron Mortensen —a police officer for 16 months, a husband, and the father of a two-year-old daughter—was arrested when he reported for duty at the Southwest Area Command. He was charged with first-degree murder and jailed in lieu of $500,000 bail.

The case had been solved with surprising swiftness, but that wasn't the focus of the media. Cop killers get a lot of ink; killer cops get even more. On top of that, Mortensen's attorney immediately went on the attack, questioning the police handling of the investigation. He raised the propriety of allowing Brady's father to sit in on his son's interview with Detective Becker. He revealed what his defense strategy would be, suggesting that Brady was actually the shooter and there was a police conspiracy to protect him because of his father's many years of service.

Adding to the controversy was the decision not to charge Brady. Activists for minority groups voiced their displeasure, alleging that if the driver of a vehicle involved in a fatal shooting were black or Hispanic, he'd most certainly be in jail.

The case went to trial in May 1997. Chris Brady, the key prosecution witness, held to his earlier police statements and grand-jury testimony about the events surrounding the killing of Daniel Mendoza.

Jurors heard a much different story when Mortensen took the stand on May 7. The defendant's version agreed with Brady's in some respects: They'd been drinking prior to the incident; the fatal bullet was fired from Mortensen's gun; they weren't initially aware that anyone had been hurt. Otherwise, their accounts were almost directly opposite. According to Mortensen, Brady drove into the alley of his own volition. When he spotted the Mendoza group, Brady tried to motion them closer to the truck. Mortensen tried to get Brady to leave the alley before shots were fired, but Brady refused. He slid across the seat, elbowed Mortensen in the chest, took his gun, and began firing.

Mortensen contended that when they learned someone had been killed, he and Brady planned to go and talk to detectives together. When he drove to Brady's apartment, he saw Brady's father in the parking lot and concluded he was being set up.

The jury apparently didn't find Mortensen's testimony credible, convicting him of first-degree murder on May 14. In the penalty phase the next day, he was sentenced to life in prison without the possibility of parole.

The conviction wasn't the end of the case for either Mortensen or Brady. The Mendoza family filed civil lawsuits and the FBI investigated possible violations of Daniel Mendoza's civil rights.

In August 1999, Christopher Brady pled guilty to federal charges of conspiracy to violate civil rights. The agreement called for Brady to serve nine years in a federal prison without consideration for parole. His attorney explained the rationale for entering a guilty plea: There was little doubt that an indictment was inevitable and Brady faced the possibility of a life sentence if found guilty at trial. Prosecutors would almost certainly have won a conviction based on Brady's admission in state court that he had gone to the McKellar Circle area to harass perceived gang members or drug dealers. The charge he pled to did not directly implicate him in the death of Daniel Mendoza.

In a *Review-Journal* article after the Mortensen verdict, Sheriff Jerry Keller is quoted

---

In 1998, Clark County had 1,255,200 residents; Metro's jurisdictional population had increased to 962,050. Metro personnel stood at 1,748 police officers, 824 civilians, 437 correction officers and 19 correction civilians.

By December 2000, Metro's jurisdictional population had increased to 1,070,972. To serve that population the department employed 1,749 sworn officers and 874 civilians. Corrections had a staff of 548 officers and 200 civilians.

---

as saying: "I don't think the Mendoza shooting sets morale back. I think it affects it, because anytime you're a member of a proud department or team and there's a little bit of tarnish, you take it personally. It's disappointing. With that disappointment, the men and women out there doing their job will be working harder to overcome all the negativity associated with this tragic, senseless incident. They'll work extra hard to prove they're not wearing a tarnished badge."

Metro's 25th

On July 1, 1998, a party was held at the MGM Grand Hotel and Casino Theme Park to celebrate Metro's 25th anniversary. The Park was closed to the public at 5 p.m. and reopened for the Metro party at 7 p.m. The event honored officers with 25 years or more of service.

Attendees were charged an admission fee of one dollar and one nonperishable food item. The cash collected resulted in a $1,600 donation to the Police Museum and more than 4,000 pounds of food was given to the Community Food Bank.

Mounted Police

In December 1998, the first Mounted Police Unit began patrolling the streets. The four-legged

Search and Rescue Officer Dies

On March 24, 1998, Officer Russell Peterson was killed while conducting a practice climb on Mt. Charleston. Climbing with a volunteer, a several-thousand-pound block of ice broke loose from the top of the mountain and hurtled down toward the two men. Barely missing the volunteer, it struck Officer Peterson, killing him instantly.

Peterson started with Metro in April 1990 and had been assigned to Search and Rescue since 1996. He was cremated and his ashes scattered over a scenic area of Mt. Charleston. Russ Peterson was survived by his wife Lesa.

members of the unit are named Buster, Nokona, Duke, and Mr. Terrible and are shod with borium shoes, which provide traction on roads and concrete surfaces. Their human partners wear riding boots and special helmets. The unit is intended to work in problem areas and at special events. It's also available to provide high visibility and deterrence in malls, business districts, and recreation areas.

Y2K

To prepare for the coming of the year 2000, Sheriff Keller formed a Y2K Task Force on February 8, 1999. Members were assigned to examine the issues relating to Y2K and to plan and prepare operational responses to any problems that might arise.

Deconsolidation Talk

Talk of splitting Metro resurfaced in September 1999. The *Las Vegas Sun* reported on September 18 that the City of Las Vegas was considering withdrawing from Metro and forming its own police department. Officials claimed that the move would save city taxpayers money—between $8 million and $15 million per year. Councilman Michael McDonald, a former Metro police officer, was quoted as saying, "I'm not satisfied with the policing we're getting and the response we're getting from the administration."

The same article quoted Sheriff Keller's response to the news. "I'm surprised they would even consider deconsolidating when they just paid $100,000 for a study that told them this is the best police department in the country." The study Keller referred to was done by DMG-Maximus. Released in March, it ranked Metro as one of the best departments the auditing firm had examined.

Controversy swirled around the deconsolidation effort for three weeks, with supporters on both sides speaking out. The backers of Metro included former governors Mike O'Callaghan and Bob Miller and former Sheriff Ralph Lamb. Councilman Michael McDonald was an advocate of the deconsolidation movement.

On the morning of October 6, hundreds of Metro employees picketed City Hall, carrying signs and wearing T-shirts with messages discouraging deconsolidation. They wanted the city to make a decision on the issue and many said that their calls to the City Council to discuss the situation were not returned. Emotions were running high, a fact that was not lost on the city officials.

On October 8, the *Sun* reported that the City of Las Vegas had scrapped its efforts to withdraw from Metro. "Deconsolidation is a non-issue," Mayor Goodman announced. "It is a dead issue. It is something that wherever it came from—it's over." The news spread quickly; it was greeted with cheers in Metro squad rooms and smiles of relief in Clark County offices.

Perhaps this time the deconsolidation matter is dead for good.

Police Officer of the Year

On December 5, 1999, three gunmen attempted to rob Mr. D's Sports Bar at the intersection of Rainbow and Oakey boulevards. The establishment was crowded with people who had been listening to the live band, Pigs in a Blanket. Had the robbers properly cased the place, they'd have known that the band was made up mostly of police officers. Some of the spectators were their off-duty co-workers.

According to an article in the *Review-Journal*, at 1:22 a.m. three men entered the back door of the Dallas Cowboys-themed bar at 1810 South Rainbow Boulevard. The band was busy putting away its equipment. A female employee of Mr. D's said she first became aware that something was wrong when one of the men tried to jump over the bar, presumably to get to the cash register. A patron pulled the man back and a few seconds later bullets began to fly. When the smoke cleared, one of the

would-be robbers was dead and five patrons were wounded, including off-duty Officer Dennis Devitte, a 20-year veteran.

Devitte had been in the bar only a short time and was engaged in a conversation with some friends when he noticed a disturbance at the end of the bar. Suddenly, gunfire erupted. Devitte saw a patron in a wheelchair struck in the shoulder by one of the bullets from the thief's 40-caliber semi-automatic. Realizing he had to act, Officer Devitte pulled his off-duty weapon, a 25-caliber handgun. Knowing he needed to be close to his target to assure accuracy, he advanced toward the gunman he had seen firing. Only a few feet apart, the cop and robber blazed away at each other. Devitte was struck a total of eight times, one round blowing out his knee. Before he

Dennis Devitte

141

fell, Devitte put eight bullets in a tight pattern in the gunman's chest. Security-tape footage showed that Devitte twice attempted to get back on his feet, but each time the injury to his knee forced him back down. The wounded gunman, Emilio Rodriguez, and his two associates fled into the parking lot, where Rodriguez collapsed and expired.

Officer Devitte survived his wounds. For his heroic actions, the International Association of Chiefs of Police honored him as Police Officer of the Year during their 2000 convention in Washington, D.C. Larry Smith, managing editor of *Parade* magazine, presented his award to him. Additionally, Officer Devitte was named "Top Cop of the Year" by the National Association of Police Officers.

Discipline

In January 2001, Metro implemented a disciplinary matrix for use by the department. Applying to both sworn and civilian personnel, the guidelines were developed in 2000 by a committee of experienced leaders, including captains, lieutenants, and civilian supervisors. The committee used three criteria: that the discipline be reasonable, fit the misconduct, and allow supervisors flexibility to use their discretion.

Under the new policy, known as a disciplinary decision guide, the punishment for violating any of 41 internal Las Vegas police rules is spelled out in writing. The new setup differs from previous police procedure, which gave the sheriff and police supervisors much more leeway in determining punishment. Now, any Las Vegas police officer who drives under the influence, lies to investigators, or commits other infractions faces stiffer penalties under the new disciplinary policy.

For example, the new rules require that any officer who lies to an Internal Affairs Bureau investigator be fired. Previously, the discipline was more subjective and could vary from case to case.

However, some officers said the punishment for lying to internal investigators was hypocritical. To bolster their claim, they cited the case of a lieutenant who had been found to have lied during an investigation of sexual harassment at the department's Personnel Bureau.

Richard Winget

The lieutenant received a 40-hour suspension for his misconduct. Afterwards, he was promoted to captain.

Undersheriff Richard Winget defended the policy. He said it was unfair to cite old cases under the new policy. He did acknowledge that if the same circumstances had occurred now, the lieutenant would have been terminated.

In spite of the concerns voiced by the unions representing the police officers and civilian employees, the administration remained steadfast. Winget said the new policy could help the department get rid of bad apples, officers who had shown a reckless disregard for the rules. "Some won't understand it and won't accept it," Winget admitted. "Luckily, the reasonable ones are the vast majority."

Remembering September 11

The terrorist attacks in New York City and Washington, D.C. and the thwarted attempt ending in a field in Pennsylvania on September 11, 2001, shocked and angered the nation. First responders—police, fire, and rescue personnel—from across the country mourned their colleagues who made the supreme sacrifice that day.

On October 4, 2001, the dead were honored in a Las Vegas ceremony, at the Police Memorial Park located at West Cheyenne and Conquistador Way. The *Review-Journal* described the scene:

"As the sun set over the mountains of Las Vegas and a police bugler sounded 'Taps,' Jean Kahre Swartz tied a blue ribbon around the branch of an ash tree. In the newly dedicated Police Memorial Park, the tree is a memorial to her son, Marc Kahre, who died on October 11, 1988. 'I think the last three weeks have made a tremendous difference in the way the public thinks of police officers,' Swartz said. 'I don't think they had the respect of a lot of people until the recent tragedies.'"

More than 100 police officers representing all major law enforcement agencies in Clark County and several local politicians attended the event.

Sheriff Jerry Keller said, "The actions of the police officers and firefighters who died in the attacks represent the height of courage and the ultimate sacrifice. They gave their lives for people they never met."

Las Vegas Mayor Oscar Goodman extended his gratitude to all the officers present. "I'm very proud," he said. "Las Vegas is a very special place. I'm thankful for the service that we receive from the people in law enforcement who put their lives on the line every day."

Ceremonies concluded with a multi-agency honor guard and a police bagpiper leading the crowd into the grove of ash trees to tie ribbons on the branches. The procession was followed by a 21-gun salute.

Shootout

Officer Enrique Hernandez lives on the northwest side of town with his wife Leean and their young daughter Maricela. The former Marine graduated from the police academy in June 2002 and finished riding with a field-training officer that October. He was at the beginning of what appeared to be a promising law-enforcement career. In March 2003, the 28-year-old talked about the incident that nearly took his life.

It happened on December 12, 2002, when Officer Hernandez was working alone on patrol on the 3 p.m. to 1 a.m. shift. At about 10:20, he was stopped at a traffic light at the intersection of Eastern and Bonanza. Facing southbound on Eastern, he observed a dark-colored SUV turn from Bonanza onto Eastern, also heading south. The vehicle had no license plate, nor was any permit, sticker, or decal visible. Immediately after making the turn, the SUV pulled into a gas station and convenience store located on the southeast corner of the intersection. As the traffic light changed, Officer Hernandez proceeded through the intersection and followed the suspect vehicle into the parking lot. He turned on his car's roof lights, planning to stop the vehicle and determine its registration status.

Although many police officers might argue that there is no such thing as a "routine" traffic stop, up to this point nothing had happened to cause the officer to become alarmed. There was no indication that there was anything particularly unusual or dangerous about the SUV or, more precisely, its driver, Javier Duarte Chavez, a 24-year-old illegal immigrant. Previously convicted of a felony in Nevada, Chavez had served time in the state prison system and been deported to Mexico upon his release. At that time, he'd been warned that he'd be in big trouble if he returned to the United States. In spite of that, he did come back, using the alias of Saul Morales Garcia. He told family and friends that he would never again go to prison or be sent back across the border.

Enrique Hernandez

That wasn't Chavez' only problem, however. On this night he was driving back from the residence of a man and woman who owed him money and were refusing to pay. Though armed with a stolen .38 revolver, the slight five-foot Mexican left the couple's home without the money after being told the police had been called.

It will never be known for sure whether Chavez thought the police were trying to stop him for the incident that had just occurred, although that seems like a strong possibility. Whatever was in his mind, he had no intention of let-

ting Officer Hernandez get a hold of him.

The lives of both men were changed drastically by the events of the next two minutes and 45 seconds.

"I put my lights on, but the SUV swung around out of the parking lot and headed back south on Eastern. I called in that I was in a pursuit and gave the direction of travel. The suspect made a left on Cedar, a right on 28th Street, and then a left on Marlin. He started out with a lead on me, but I was gaining on him all the time," Hernandez remembers.

"Shortly after we got on Marlin, he lost control of the vehicle, jumped the curb and hit a light pole. I pulled in to the curb behind him. He hit that pole pretty hard and I didn't think he'd get out and run right away, but he did. I called in that I was now in a foot pursuit and the chase was on again.

"We were running through an apartment complex and I was several yards behind. All of a sudden I saw one of the apartment doors open and he ran inside, the door shut behind him. He hadn't displayed a weapon yet, but it was obvious there was more to this than I had originally thought. In my mind, I was concerned that he may take the occupants of the apartment hostage. I drew my gun, opened the door, and went in. I didn't see the suspect, but there was a woman standing inside the door and a couple of little kids. The woman started screaming.

"It was a small apartment. The living room was on my right and I could see that the next room toward the back was a kitchen area, with a sliding glass door leading to the outside. I didn't know if the suspect had gone out the back or was somewhere in the apartment. I started moving cautiously toward the kitchen, stopping by the wall that separated the two rooms. As I again went forward into the kitchen, I detected movement against the wall to my left, about five feet away. Then I saw two muzzle flashes. My left arm was jerked back, but I didn't realize right away that I'd been hit. We then fired at each other simultaneously. I learned later that my round struck him near the right armpit and exited out his back. His bullet got me in my right forearm, my gun arm. It shattered the bone, then traveled up my arm and lodged in my shoulder; it's still in there. It felt like the arm had been blown off. It went dead and I lost the feeling in it; my gun fell out of my hand to the floor. I was now totally defenseless. It turned out that his wound wasn't debilitating."

There was a brief pause, during which Officer Hernandez realized that he had to get out of that apartment. As he started to

retreat he accidentally kicked his gun, knocking it under a piece of furniture. Before he could get out of the room, Chavez again opened fire. Hernandez was struck in his side, neck, and leg. He stumbled toward the front door, falling, then regaining his feet. He made it outside and fell to the ground about 10 feet from the door. Chavez, his gun now empty, fled in the other direction through the sliding-glass doors. It was later learned that the apartment in which the shooting occurred was where Chavez lived. The screaming woman was his girlfriend.

Hernandez continued his story, "A guy came out of the apartment and asked if I was okay and told me not to die. It turned out that he was the suspect's brother-in-law. He'd been upstairs taking a shower while the shooting was going on. I asked him to call 9-1-1 and tell them what had happened. The last they'd heard from me was when I called in the foot pursuit. Responding units would have no idea exactly where I was."

As additional personnel arrived, they administered medical treatment while Hernandez, who remained conscious at all times, provided suspect information. He said it wasn't until he got into the ambulance that the pain began to set in.

While the fallen officer was being transported to the hospital, his survival uncertain, the hunt for Javier Duarte Chavez began. SWAT and K-9 teams soon tracked the fugitive to a nearby row of unoccupied apartments. One of the dogs confirmed that Chavez was hiding in an air-shaft a few feet above the floor. As SWAT officers prepared to enter the apartment, they were not certain of how much ammunition Chavez had for the .38, and thought he might have picked up Hernandez' service weapon, which remained undiscovered at the scene of the shooting.

After several unsuccessful attempts to get Chavez to surrender, he pointed his .38 at the officers and they opened fire, killing the suspect. It was later determined that his gun had been empty and the incident was a case of "suicide by cop." A coroner's inquest and Use of Force Board both ruled that the shooting of Chavez was justified.

Officer Hernandez was released from the hospital before Christmas, but he faced more than a year of therapy and rehabilitation. In January 2004 he completed treatment and was taken off medication. He retuned to work on light-duty at the Downtown Area Command and the Public Information Office. In early March he was assigned to the Domestic Violence Detail on restricted duty. He carries a gun, but is prohibited from getting in-volved in physical altercations. It is anticipated that the three bullets still in his body will eventually work themselves out and no surgery is planned. "My right arm is in good shape. My hand is only about 60% and my left foot hurts most of the time, but I'm back to work and I'm happy," Enrique says. He has no complaints about how Metro has treated him since the shooting.

"I couldn't ask for anything more. My Metro family has done everything possible in the way of help and support," he said.

And finally, the big question. On that night, wounded and unarmed, did he think he was going to die?

"I never thought that. I knew I was going to live," Hernandez said confidently.

Under those circumstances, how could he be so sure?

"Because I wasn't going to let a guy like him kill me."

And he didn't.

Keller Retires

In a December 2002 interview, Sheriff Keller commented on his philosophy for running Metro.

"A police department is only as good as the trust placed in it by the public. I'm a strong believer in community policing," he said. "Public outreach, interaction between the police and the public, is critical to establishing that trust."

The programs Keller initiated reflect his commitment to those beliefs. In February 1995, "First Tuesday" was launched. On the first Tuesday of each month, citizens are invited to visit their area command headquarters to meet with officers and discuss their concerns. Two radio shows—Partners with the Community and Police Officers Promoting Unity—were introduced. In addition, he implemented the Victim-Witness Program, Domestic Violence Unit, Citizen Youth Academy, Drug Intervention Combined Enforcement, and the Local Chiefs Committee-Partners in Law Enforcement.

Promoting community policing was not the only ingredient necessary for success, however. "Hiring and developing quality people is key. The most well-intentioned programs won't work without the right personnel," Keller said.

Results indicate Metro does in fact have the right people in the right places. A 40% decrease in crime over the last eight years is one of the more striking statistics cited by Keller. "And I love working with these people. I look forward to coming to work every day because of them," he added.

Is there anything facing the department or community that causes him major concern?

"Club drugs are a real problem. People don't fully appreciate the dangers of these drugs."

How about the terrorist attacks that occurred on September 11, 2001? What impact did they have on Metro?

"The best terrorist attack is the one that never happens, of course. I can't comment on specific details, but Clark County is beyond the response planning stage and into prevention. Unfortunately, some communities are still in the process of figuring out what to do after something happens. We have a tremendous working relationship with other federal, state, and local agencies. There is more to be done, but we're making good progress," he said.

How did Clark County move from response to prevention planning in such a relatively short time?

"Y2K. Had the terrorists struck in 1999, it would have been much more difficult for first responders to prepare for future attacks. If you recall, leading up to 2000 there was rampant speculation that computer systems would fail nationwide. Municipalities would lose their power, water, sewage, and telephone service. All across America, government officials had to develop plans to deal with these things. Because of that, our responses to those scenarios were substantially in place before 9/11."

Was there any particular reason he decided not to run for another term?

"Quite frankly, I didn't feel that I could run a political campaign and give the necessary attention to getting our anti-terror efforts up to speed at the same time. Protecting this community is my top priority, so I decided to bow out of contention and devote my time to where it mattered most."

Sheriff Keller left office in January 2003.

Sheriff Bill Young

In January 2003, Bill Young was sworn in as Clark County Sheriff. A native Nevadan, Young was born in Yerington and moved to Las Vegas as a child. He's a 1974 graduate of Bishop Gorman High School and has a Bachelor of Arts degree from UNLV. He is married and has four children.

Sheriff Young began his career with Metro in 1979. In 1984 he was promoted to sergeant and served in Patrol, Field Training, and SWAT. After attaining the rank of lieutenant in 1986, he was again assigned to Patrol, and also served as Operations Manager of the Communications Center and in Vice/Narcotics. He again took a step up the ladder in 1995 when he was promoted to captain. Young commanded the Support Services Bureau, overseeing the Resident Officer, K-9, Air Support, and Search and Rescue programs. After being elevated to deputy chief in January 1999, he was assigned to the Detention Services Division;

Bill Young

he then took over the Special Operations Division in February 2001.

In a March 2003 interview, Sheriff Young discussed the current status of Metro and his plans for the future of the department.

"The lingering economic effects of the terrorist attacks of September 11 (2001) continue to be a problem we have to deal with," Young said. "We have to do more with less and the federal money isn't coming in."

However, Young is optimistic that Metro has the wherewithal to deal with difficult financial times and maintain the level of service and protection the residents of Metro's jurisdiction have become accustomed to. He plans on keeping the ratio of officers to jurisdictional population at two per 1,000, even as the population numbers continue to increase.

Regarding the future, "I want to make sure the department is well-positioned for the next ten to fifteen years down the road," Young said. "I want to be certain that we have sufficient numbers of personnel and jail space to get criminals off the streets and keep them off the streets. Las Vegas and Clark County must continue to be safe for residents and tourists alike."

When Sheriff Young took office, he directed the Training Bureau to develop a method for bringing important information to Metro's officers quickly. Such information includes vehicle pursuits—one of the most dangerous situations an officer can face, both in terms of physical danger and liability—and use of force, criminal law, and search and seizure.

As a result of the sheriff's directive, the Metro Educational Training System (METS) was introduced in March 2003. Through METS, consistent updates on policy, procedure, and techniques are presented to officers by supervisors at the unit or squad level. These updates may take the form of lesson plans, Power Point presentations, or videos and are presented weekly.

Another area that caught Sheriff Young's attention was the 9-1-1 Communications Bureau. He learned that the unprecedented population growth in Las Vegas and Clark County had placed a tremendous burden on the emergency-communications system. Callers requesting assistance were experiencing waits of two minutes or longer for their calls to be processed. This was a situation Young found to be potentially dangerous and unacceptable.

To help remedy the problem, he approved a plan that assigned officers who were on temporary light-duty status to work in the communications center. The duties performed by these officers include taking phone calls that require an officer's expertise, but not necessarily a response by a field unit, and providing advice and answering questions about the reporting of non-violent crimes.

According to Captain Mark Medina, Communications Bureau Commander, the light-duty officers were initially reluctant to participate in the new program. However, they soon learned that working in the communications center was fast-paced and never boring. In addition, their presence frees up additional 9-1-1 operators to exclusively handle life-threatening emergencies.

Through September 2003, 16 officers have participated in Sheriff Young's initiative. The average wait time for call processing is now down to ten seconds or less, making the program a winner for both the department and the public.

Although it's still too early in his administration to have meaningful statistics to reference, Sheriff Young's dedication to his task should be reassuring to those who reside in, or plan to visit, Las Vegas.

7

Recollections

The Cowboy Cop

Hiram "Hi" Powell worked for both of the agencies that would subsequently merge to form Metro. He began his law-enforcement career in 1942 with the Las Vegas Police Department and later moved to the Clark County Sheriff's Department. He retired from there in 1967, with a total of 25 years of service.

Powell came to Las Vegas in 1940 from Electra, Texas, to participate in a rodeo. Twenty years old at the time, his forté was bronco riding. After the event, he remained in town. "I never had enough money to leave," he recalls.

Powell gave up his bronco-busting efforts soon after and found work in the construction business. He tried his hand as a deputy sheriff in 1941 and was assigned to work

Hiram Powell

foot patrol in Pittman (now a part of Henderson).

"There was nothing but bars, construction workers, and fights," is how Powell remembers that assignment. He worked alone and had no radio contact with the department. If he needed a car to transport an arrestee or if he needed backup, he had to get to a telephone and call in the request. That sometimes proved a difficult task if he was in a tussle with a group of rowdy drunks.

After about three months, Powell told the sheriff that he either had to be given some help or he'd have to leave. With no money in the budget to hire additional personnel, the sheriff said the Las Vegas Police Department was hiring and suggested Powell apply there.

At that time, the LVPD was located on Second Street, right behind the Apache Hotel. The facility included a courtroom, records section, and male and female jails. The men's jail was known as the Blue Room and the females were housed in the Pink Room.

Powell's first meeting with Chief of Police Don Borax didn't go very well. The two men got into an argument in the chief's office and a shouting match ensued. "I don't need this goddamn job anyway," the Texan said and started for the door.

Before he could make it across the room, Borax called to him. Powell spun around, ready for more verbal battle. Instead, Borax asked, "Can you start at eight tomorrow morning?"

Thus began Hi Powell's sometimes frustrating, sometimes tempestuous, but always rewarding career.

When Powell joined the force, it had about 20 officers. The population of Las Vegas was around 10,000. His blue uniform was furnished, along with a badge and identification card. Officers provided their own guns and leather.

"It was a real poor department," he says. "They were short of patrol cars. We had to ride for two hours, then walk for two hours while somebody else used the car."

The department had no portable radios in those days. However, that didn't mean that the cops patrolling the downtown area on foot were without any means of communication. In fact, the officers had a unique way of finding out if the station needed to reach them. A red light was mounted on top of the Apache Hotel and wired to the station. When the light came on, the patrolman had to call in for his message or assignment. Of course, the efficiency of the system depended on the patrolmen remembering to check the red light from time to time.

"The job was very political back then. The chief served at the pleasure of the mayor and City Council. If they didn't like the way he parted his hair, they got rid of him," Powell says. "And every time they fired one, they'd put in what they called an 'acting' chief. Some of those guys served as chief three or four different times. I think I worked for nine chiefs in nine years."

The politics of the job frequently got Powell into trouble. People with political connections expected to be left alone by the police. If they weren't, they didn't hesitate to call their contact and complain. This was a problem that dogged him throughout his tenure with the LVPD. As an example, he cites his stormy relationship with one such character: Benjamin "Bugsy" Siegel.

Powell recalls his first meeting with the notorious gangster: "It was in the mid 1940s, probably '46 or '47. It was early in the morning, and it was in the winter. I remember it being cold and windy. I stopped Siegel for a traffic infraction at East Charleston and Fifth Street. When he handed me his license, there was a $100 bill folded up with it. That was a lot of money at the time, but I dropped the bill on the ground. The last I saw of it, it was blowing down East Charleston. I gave Siegel his ticket and let him go.

"About an hour later I got a radio message to return to the station and report to the chief, George Thompson. He asked me what happened between Siegel and me. After I told him, he fired me. I turned in my badge and ID and went home.

"The next morning Thompson called and asked me to come back to work. He said we had to forget about the past. I told him I didn't have a badge or ID and hung up. A half-hour later he was at my place with my stuff. About a week after that I ran into Siegel and two of his bodyguards outside the Western Union on Fremont Street. Siegel said something about having shown me who was the boss. That didn't set real well with me, so I slapped the hell out of him. I asked his bodyguards if they wanted a piece of me, but they all took off."

Surprisingly, there were no repercussions over the incident. But a couple of weeks later, Powell got a call from Rex Bell, who owned a western clothing store on Fremont Street. He said he had something at the store for him and asked him to stop by.

The item Bell had was a new white Stetson hat. "I knew I hadn't ordered a hat, and I would never order a white one. I asked Bell who paid for it. He said it was compliments of Bugsy Siegel. I took the hat and drove out to the Flamingo. I found Siegel in the blackjack pit talking to the pit boss. I put the hat on him and shoved it down over his ears. I told him: 'You bought it—you wear it.' Then I turned around and walked out."

Powell had his share of difficulties in dealing with the lesser-known hoodlums, too. He liked to roust them and try to get them out of town. These encounters often resulted in his being called on the carpet by the chief. Not one to concede to the bad guys, he came up with a way around the problem.

"I'd get up real early, around two o'clock or so, and take a ride downtown. I'd round up a couple of the hoods and take them to jail. But I had a deal worked out with the jailer that these guys wouldn't get booked. He'd hold them until dawn and then turn them loose. There was no record that they were ever in the jail. With any luck, they'd grab the next transportation out of town when they got out.

"I eventually got called on that, too. When the chief asked me about it, I denied everything. I asked him where the records were that said I was arresting these guys. Of course, there weren't any. I wasn't really arresting them anyway; I was just rousting them. But you could do a lot of things back then that you could never do now."

To get away from the politics of the LVPD, Powell switched uniforms in the early 1950s and went back to work for the Clark County Sheriff's Department. By then, a public-employee retirement system was in place that allowed him to make the move without losing any of his service time. Although the actual job of policing was pretty much the same, working for an elected official made all the difference.

After retiring from policing, Hi Powell went back to work for Metro as a part-time civilian employee, assigned in the Detective Division at the City Hall complex. He completely retired in 2003 at the age of 83.

The Wild West

H. Don Rowe was born in Kansas in 1925. When he was 14, he moved with his family to Santa Monica, California. During World War II, he served aboard a destroyer in the Pacific. Discharged in 1946, he moved to Las Vegas, where his first job was as an attendant in a Texaco station at Fifth Street and Fremont. In January 1947 at age 21, he was hired by the Las Vegas Police Department.

The police station was then located on North Second Street. "It was just an adobe building with a corrugated metal roof and no insulation. The Blue Room had a dirt floor," he recalls.

There was no training academy in those days either. New cops

Don Rowe

learned the ropes on the streets. "The day I started, an inspector handed me my badge and said: 'Here you are, prick.' I guess I looked at him kind of funny. He started to laugh and said: 'Well, that's what they think you are as soon as you pin it on.' It wasn't long before I knew what he meant," Rowe says.

"The city ended at the El Cortez, and we only had a total of two traffic lights in town. One was at Fifth and Fremont; the other was at Main and Fremont. They were both always on flash," Rowe remembers Las Vegas at the time. "It's hard to imagine that today."

In February, with just over a month on the job, Rowe was working the graveyard shift with another officer. "It was about one o'clock and colder than hell. We were going to a restaurant to get a cup of coffee; the other guy was driving. We were going past a filling station at Fifth and Carson when all of a sudden my partner pulls out his gun and puts it on his lap. 'Get ready for trouble,' he says.

"I didn't know what he was talking about, but I drew my gun too. He pulled into that filling station and we could see two guys talking in the office. He told me to go check them out. As soon as I opened the car door, one of the guys left the office and approached me. He was wearing a heavy coat and his hands were in his pockets. I asked if he worked there and he said no. When I told him to get his hands out of his pockets, he fired at me through his jacket. He missed.

"I grabbed his arm so he couldn't get his gun out and get a better shot. He grabbed my gun hand and got hold of the cylinder, blocking it so I couldn't fire. In that position, we danced toward Carson. He eventually got his gun free and fired again. This time he got me in the left forearm. It broke bone and knocked me on my ass. When I looked up, he was running away. I fired and must have grazed him. He went down, but got right back up and took off."

It turned out that Rowe and his partner had stumbled across

an armed robbery in progress. The second man in the office when they pulled into the station was the proprietor. Although Clark County Sheriff's units responded to assist, the suspect got away.

"I heard that the FBI killed the guy in Louisiana about three years later. He'd escaped from prison, I think in New Mexico, and was a fugitive. I never found out for sure if that was true, but that's what I heard," Rowe says.

"Did my partner do anything wrong during that incident? I'm not going to say. But I can tell you this: He was fired the next day."

Rowe believed he was the second LVPD officer to be shot in the line of duty. The first was Ernest May, who was shot and killed in 1933.

Officer Rowe recovered from his injuries and returned to work about seven months later. He was assigned to work foot patrol down-

town on the afternoon shift. This was a one-man detail.

"There really wasn't a lot of crime then. There wasn't a drug problem and no prostitutes were walking the streets either. Roxie's whorehouse was the only joint in town and that was located four miles out on Boulder Highway. In fact, they sometimes referred to the place as Four Mile. And they ran the place tight; there were no problems out there. The main thing we had to deal with in the city was drunks and fights," according to Rowe. "We didn't have radios and backup wasn't even part of our vo-

Roxie Clippenger and her husband

Roxie's (Four Mile) (left)

cabulary. You had to rely on yourself and your fists."

Friday nights were when the cowboys would come to town. They worked at ranches within a few miles of Las Vegas and rode their horses in to do some drinking and let off a little steam. After tying their mounts to one

Busting Roxie's in the '50s

of the hitching posts on the street, they went into a bar and had at it. Most of them did their drinking in the saloons on First Street. Conveniently, these establishments were only about a half-block from the jail.

"They were really pretty nice guys," Rowe opines. "But they liked to drink, and when they got drunk they loved to fight."

The usual Friday night went something like this. By 7:30 or so, the cowboys were feeling their drinks. That's about when the fights started. Unfortunately for the cops, the rowdies didn't limit their altercations to other like-minded individuals. The police uniform often attracted more trouble than it deterred.

"I'd be making my rounds and walking in and out of the saloons. It wouldn't be long before someone would holler: 'Hey Rowe! I think I

can kick your ass.' They'd walk over to me and the fight would be on," Rowe recalls.

Officer Rowe developed a strategy that proved very effective in these situations. "When the guy was getting ready to swing, I'd deck him," Rowe says. He'd then reach down and grab the unconscious challenger and drag him down the alley to the jail.

The next morning, Rowe appeared when the offender was taken before the judge. "A lot of the time they'd ask me what I hit them with. I'd tell them it was just my fist. They'd smile and offer to buy me a drink next time they saw me. There was no animosity; nobody held a grudge," he says.

What was Officer Rowe's scariest situation while with the LVPD?

"It wasn't the gunfight or any of my battles with the drunks," he says. "In fact, there were actually two incidents that really got to me, and they both involved mortuaries.

"The first one was just after I joined the force, before the gunfight even. I was working the afternoon shift with another guy. It was getting late, around eleven or so, and my partner wanted to stop in to see a buddy of his at the Bunker Mortuary on Stewart and Fifth. We went in the back door and were in a room where they kept caskets and stuff. The embalming was done in the next room. The door to that room was open and there was only a bluish nightlight on. I could see there were two stiffs on the slabs, covered with sheets. The whole place reeked of formaldehyde. The smell, caskets, bodies, and that eerie blue light had me kind of edgy.

"I was standing in the doorway to the embalming room, listening to my partner and Lee, the mortician, talk. All of a sudden, one of the stiffs sits straight up and lets out a groan. Well, my gun was in my hand in a flash and I drew down on the corpse. I stopped myself before I pulled the trigger, but I came within a whisker of shooting the dead guy.

"I can't tell you to this day why I pulled my gun. I guess I was just scared. Lee and my partner thought it was one of the funniest things they'd ever seen. I didn't find it the least bit amusing, at least not at the time.

"After he stopped laughing, Lee explained that the guy had only been dead a few hours. His stomach muscles contracted, causing him to sit up. When that happened, the air left in his lungs was forced out, causing what sounded like a groan.

"The second time was a couple years later, in 1949 I think. This time I was the veteran and I had a new kid working with me. There had been a real bad car accident earlier in the day; five people had been killed out past the Flamingo.

"Anyway, it was another afternoon shift and it was getting late. Palm Mortuary was located at First and Carson and I wanted to see the guy who ran the place about something or other. The rookie and I go in the front door. The place is very dimly lit, just a couple of nightlights on. We walk into the back and there are six stiffs: three on gurneys, two on the slabs, and another one on a couch, all covered with sheets. Palm had gotten all the accident victims and apparently had an extra one besides.

"I called out for the mortician. Just then, the damn stiff on the couch sits up and says: 'What do you want?'

"It turned out that the guy I wanted to talk with had decided to catch some sleep and laid down in there with the bodies, and covered himself all up in a sheet. Well, I want to tell you, there were two cops who came real, real close to needing a change of uniforms.

"The rookie thought it was all a setup and he cursed me out real good. I don't think he ever forgave me, or believed that I was just as scared as he was."

How about his fondest memory of those early days?

"Helldorado Days, no doubt about it," Rowe says.

Helldorado Days

Started in 1934, Helldorado Days was an annual event sponsored by the Elk's Club. Each May for three or four days, Las Vegas put on its party hat and celebrated. "It was the highlight of the year. It drew tourists, sure, but the locals really looked forward to it."

"There was always a Sunday parade. They had floats pulled by horses and the showgirls from the Strip hotels would get all dressed up and ride on them. There were mounted posses with some of the most beautiful saddles you'd ever want to see, marching bands and clowns, too. A lot of western movie actors made appearances. Some of the best-known stars of the day, like Gene Autry and Leo Carrillo, showed up.

"The parade started on Main, went up Fremont, and ended around Eleventh or Twelfth Street. It drew huge crowds and there were an awful lot of kids. It was fun, just plain fun," Rowe says.

"Then there was Helldorado Village, located at Fifth and Bonanza. It was built just like an old cavalry fort and covered at least half a block. It had big wooden gates and on the grounds there were food stands, rides for the kids, and a dance hall for the adults.

"They even had the big steel-barred cell from the Blue Room brought to Fremont Street. Anybody not wearing one of the Helldorado badges sold by the Elk's Club would be arrested and put in that cell. They'd stay in there until somebody paid cash money for their fine, too," Rowe laughs.

"They had all kinds of contests. I remember guys would stop shaving about five months ahead of time so they could compete for the best-beard award. Like I said, it was just a fun time. And the thing about it, there was no big increase in crime. There was the usual stuff involving people having too much to drink, but that was about as far as it went.

"If I could turn the clock back right now, that's where I'd take it. That was the fun Las Vegas and that's where I'd want to be."

Rowe quit the LVPD in late 1951 and returned to Santa Monica. "The job was too political; you could get fired any time for any reason. That went for chiefs and officers both, it didn't make any difference."

In 1954, Rowe went through the Motor Academy and worked in Traffic in California for some time. He returned to Las Vegas in 1958. While attending the University of Nevada in 1962, he went to work for the Clark County Sheriff's Department. During his time in the CCSD and subsequently the LVMPD, he attained the rank of lieutenant. He served in the jail and as a Field Lieutenant; his last position was as Watch Commander on the swing shift.

Lieutenant Rowe retired in 1984 with 29 years of dedicated service.

A Minority View

Herman Moody was born in Louisiana in 1924 and raised in McNary, Arizona. He and his family moved to Las Vegas in 1940. Herman finished high school in 1943 and was drafted into the Navy. He was discharged in 1946 after serving in various campaigns in the Pacific and Aleutian Islands. Returning to Las Vegas, he was awaiting admission to a diesel-engineering class in Los Angeles when Inspector Chuck Morris of the LVPD recruited him. Morris told Moody that the department had a need for African-American officers and asked him to consider a career in law enforcement. The 22-year-old joined the LVPD in November 1946.

At that time there was only one other African-American officer, Joe Harris, on the force. Moody was partnered with him and they were assigned to work Westside, where the majority of blacks in Las Vegas resided.

"Our area ran from Bonanza to Harrison and from A to H streets. There were some white, Indian, and Mexican families living in that neighborhood, too. They were good people," Moody recalls.

"There wasn't a lot of street crime then. Most of our calls were domestics, family fights and things like that," he says. "Nobody ever told me that I was assigned there because of the black population, but it was pretty easy to figure out."

After two or three weeks, Harris took ill and Herman found himself out on the streets alone. "I'd stop over to his house, let him know what was going on and get advice," Herman explains.

How did the various ethnic groups he policed receive him?

"I never had any problems because of anybody's race, not mine or theirs. I treated people with respect and that's the way they treated me.

Herman Moody

As long as I was fair with them, we got along fine."

Working Westside was a pretty easy job, huh?

"I didn't say that," Moody grins mischievously. "Sometimes the fights with the drunks got pretty nasty. I remember there was this bar called the Westside Tavern at A and Wilson streets. The Indians used to go there and get their whiskey. When they got real drunk, there'd be some ugly brawls. The owner of the place complained that when one of those things broke out, he was so busy defending his own life and property that he didn't have time to call the police. So we worked out a way for him to let us know if there was trouble. He put three lights up on the roof of the bar. The green light meant everything was cool. The yellow light meant trouble was brewing. If the red light came on, we knew it had hit the fan and we'd better get there quick. Whenever we looked at that roof, we were hoping to see green."

How about his peers on the LVPD? How did they treat him?

"That was not a racist department. I don't know what the guys thought personally, but stuff about race wasn't a big problem on the job. The subject wasn't even talked about much, that I remember."

So being a black cop in those days was a piece of cake?

"No. It wasn't always easy, but

it was nothing I couldn't handle."

Because there was no training to speak of, officers learned from their partners, their own experiences, and through their own initiative. To make sure he was as good at his job as he could be, Moody read about the law and the police profession. He read whatever books he could find locally and sent away for others.

"I wanted to make sure I knew what I was doing. It wasn't a good idea to arrest somebody and then not be able to find any law they'd violated," he laughs.

As more black officers were hired, Moody was given the additional responsibility of coordinating their training and scheduling. Dusting off his law-enforcement books, he had the new guys over to his house a couple nights a week to share his knowledge with them.

In the early 1960s, three years after applying to be a traffic officer, the transfer was granted and Herman Moody became the first African-American motorcycle cop in LVPD history. From there, he became a detective and was among the first members of a new narcotics unit. He also saw service in the Larceny and Fugitive details.

Are there any specific incidents in his career hat still stand out in his mind?

"There are two that I can think of," Moody says. "The first

wasn't long after I started. I was in the station one night reporting for an eight-to-four shift, when this Indian comes in and says his friend is stuck in the tar pit over by the railroad tracks. They used tar to treat the railroad ties and there was a big tar pit back in off of Main Street at the time.

"He says that he and two buddies, one white and one black, were walking around back there in the dark. The white guy was in the lead, fell into the pit, and couldn't get out. The black guy stayed with the victim and sent him for help.

"As I remember it, these guys were all in their twenties and were trying to get to the Wobbly Wobbly Jungle. That was what they called the hobo camp that was in the same area. They got lost and ended up at the tar pit.

"I took the Indian in the patrol car and we went over to the pit. I had my flashlight and there was a bigger floodlight in the car. By the time we got there, the white guy was sunk in all the way up to his neck. The black kid was tall, and he was stretched out from the bank across the tar, holding his buddy's head up to keep him from drowning.

"We got the fire department out there and they got a cable around the guy to keep him from sinking any further. The trouble was, the tar was so thick that they couldn't yank him out quickly or they'd have hurt or killed him. It was a real slow process, and it took almost seven hours to get him free.

"That rescue made the national news and I believe there was a story about it in *Life* magazine.

"The second thing was when I was with Metro, so it must have been around '74 or '75. Another detective and I were out in our car when there was a radio call that an officer from a neighboring agency needed assistance. We were clear at the time and responded.

"When we got to the scene, three of the other agency's patrol cars were there. A sergeant was standing by his car and said that a mentally deranged man was behind a vehicle parked in a driveway several feet away. He said the guy was armed and had taken his weapon and those of his other two officers as well. I looked at his holster and sure enough, it was empty.

"I learned later that the three units had responded one at a time. The guy got the drop on the first officer and took his gun, and the same with the second and third. The situation when we got there was a standoff. The suspect was demanding that a judge be brought

out for him to talk with. At that point, nobody had been hurt.

I was behind our car, gun drawn, when something set the guy off. He left his cover and came toward us, a gun in each hand, saying: 'Give it up! Give it up!'

"I guess he wanted us to give him our guns. As he was coming, I had him in my sights and could have killed him right then. But something told me not to shoot. I lowered my aim to his leg and all of a sudden he opened fire. One of the officers from the other department was hit and went down. I returned fire and got him in the leg and he dropped.

"Some of the other guys rushed him and disarmed him. No more shots were fired and everybody recovered. No one was killed."

What would Herman Moody most like to be remembered for? Making history as the first black motorcycle cop in the LVPD, perhaps?

"No," he says. "I want to be remembered for what I was: a cop—just a cop."

Herman retired from Metro in November 1977, after providing more than three decades of service to the people of Las Vegas.

"Father" Ed

Edward Jensen applied to the Las Vegas Police Department in July 1970, during a recruiting sweep in his home state of Minnesota. He was hired and moved to Las Vegas that October, beginning a 29-year law-enforcement career in Clark County. In January 2003 he recalled some of his experiences during that tenure. One incident that came to mind was an undercover operation in 1976.

"I was working in Vice and Narcotics at that time. There was this guy that we suspected was responsible for a number of burglaries. We just hadn't been able to catch him. They came up with a plan for me to join up with this guy by posing as an expert on disabling burglar alarms. A local alarm company provided me with training on how to get past the alarms and then I made my move on the burglar," Jensen says.

The burglars Jensen joined consisted of the chief suspect and an assistant, both of whom were usually high on heroin. For their first

Ed Jensen (left) and Jerry Keller

job, they selected a fur store located at Sixth Street and Sahara. Jensen's superiors notified the store and an agreement was reached holding Metro responsible for any loss or damage to the merchandise. As an additional precaution, arrangements were made so that no police units would respond to the alarm, should Jensen fail in his attempt to disable it.

"When we went to go in, I took care of the alarm as planned. My two associates were so stoned that they couldn't get through the door, so I had to kick it in for them. Once we got inside, we took out armloads of expensive furs. We had the car and trunk pretty well full when we heard a siren heading our way. I wasn't sure what had happened, but I figured there might have been some kind of a screw-up or that maybe somebody passing by had seen what we were doing and called it in. Anyway, we decided to get the hell out of there."

About two blocks away they met the source of the siren: an

ambulance, totally unrelated to the burglary. The three thieves held a brief debate about going back to the store for more goodies. They decided not to press their luck and instead took the loot to their hideout, a sleazy downtown motel.

"For the next two days I kept an eye on the stuff, while my partners stayed high on their heroin and tried to figure out how to get rid of the furs. With no apparent progress being made in that regard, it was decided to close down the operation and get those furs back to their owner.

"They raided our motel and I was arrested along with the other two; I didn't get any special treatment, believe me. I was booked and went through the infamous body-cavity search," Jensen says with a smile. "Then I spent about ten hours locked up in the jail."

What Ed Jensen remembers most about his career is his long and sometimes frustrating struggle to get assistance for officers who needed help in dealing with problems, especially those having been involved n shootings.

This was an area with which Jensen had a certain amount of expertise. During his first 12 years with the Las Vegas Police Department and then Metro, Jensen was personally involved in three shootings, two of them fatal. In 1974, while he was in pursuit of a suspect

in a gas-station robbery, a shoot-out occurred and the suspect was killed. In 1978, Jensen and three other detectives stopped a vehicle suspected of being involved in a fast-food-store robbery. The driver pulled a shotgun and aimed it at the officers; all four fired. The suspect died three weeks later. In 1982, Jensen and his partner responded to a residential burglary in progress. As the suspect exited the front door of the home he pointed a gun; Jensen fired once, but missed.

During those days, Metro provided little if any assistance in helping officers deal with such traumatic experiences. Between 1982 and 1984, the Personnel Department did send involved officers to San Jose, California, for a psychological evaluation, but that was about the extent of it. Ed Jensen believed more could and should be done in the way of support. Recruiting an Internal Affairs lieutenant, Jerry Keller, to his cause, the pair began a two-year crusade to bring about the needed changes.

During the ensuing months they tried and failed, again and again, to sell their superiors on the concept of creating a support system for officers who needed help in coping with personal or job-related problems. Each time they were shot down, they came right back for more, but it wasn't always easy.

"I walked out of several meetings when they got so intense I felt like punching somebody. I let Jerry stay and use his verbal skills on them; he was really good at that," Jensen remembers.

An incident occurring almost simultaneously weighed on his mind as the battle continued. It involved a superior dismissing his suggestion for implementing another plan that would have been helpful to a specific class of citizens: prostitutes.

"My partner and I found this prostitute who wanted to get away from her pimp and return to her hometown, but she was afraid the guy would beat her. We took her to the airport and contacted her parents; they wired her a ticket good for the next day. We stayed with the girl all night and got her on the plane. Her parents wrote and thanked us for saving their daughter.

"I thought that doing something like that was not only humanitarian, but also worked to reduce crime by reducing the number of girls working the streets. I made a pitch to a superior, suggesting the department should actively encourage helping those who wanted to get away from that lifestyle. He listened, and then told me: 'You can either be a cop or a priest, but you can't be both.' That was the end of that idea."

Jensen and Keller got their big break in September 1984, when Sheriff John Moran approved starting the Police Employee Assistance Program on a six-month trial basis. The first PEAP office was on the second floor of City Hall in a room the size of a broom closet. Their only equipment was an antique telephone answering machine and they had to use their personal vehicles to get around in. It wasn't much, but it was a start. Today, that six-month trial is in its 21st year.

As time passed, calls to PEAP increased.

"It got so we were being contacted for almost every conceivable situation, including people wanting to know the best place to have a pet buried. Some of those things weren't exactly what we had intended, but that was okay. People were calling us; they felt that when they needed help, we'd be there for them. That's what counted."

In May 1999, Ed Jensen received the Award of Excellence. It stated: "In recognition and deep appreciation for your lifetime of commitment, years of personal sacrifice, the countless hearts you have touched, and most importantly, your Gift of Presence." That seems to say it all.

He retired from Metro in December 1999.

A "Special" Cop

Dwight Mahan was born in California and moved to Las Vegas in 1961. The Clark County Sheriff's Department hired him in February 1966; he retired from Metro in 2001 with 35 years of service. Mr. Mahan shared the memories of his law-enforcement career in a February 2003 interview.

"The consolidation of the two police agencies in 1973 to form Metro was certainly one of many highlights," he said.

Dwight Mahan with George Bush

"There was a lot of friction initially, but after several months everyone was wearing the same uniform, carrying the same weapons, and driving the same colored vehicles. That's when things smoothed out and we began to really function as players on the same team. The merger benefited the taxpayers and provided more efficient service to all the citizens; it was definitely the right way to go.

"Another thing I'll always remember is my service with the first SWAT teams. We started out in 1974 with officers being assigned on a part-time basis, receiving training when their other duties allowed. In 1976, we went to full-time assignments. That's when the training really picked up and started the evolution into the highly trained professional unit of today."

Is there any particular case that sticks in his mind from the SWAT days?

"Jesse Bishop. He attempted to rob the El Morocco casino just before Christmas in 1977. There happened to be a newlywed couple in the casino at the time of the robbery, and Bishop shot and killed the husband. There was a big manhunt and we caught him sleeping under a trailer in Boulder City thirty-six hours later. We took him into custody without a fight." The 46-year-old Bishop was convicted of the murder and sentenced to death. Refusing to cooperate in the appeals that were filed on his behalf by anti-death penalty advocates, he died in Nevada's gas chamber on October 22, 1979.

In 1982, Mahan, then a lieutenant, was working out of the South Area Command. Las Vegas was becoming increasingly popular as a location to film movies and hold concerts and major sporting events. At that time, off-duty officers—working for the promoter—provided services such as security and traffic control for these events. When he was assigned to organize the National Sheriff's Association convention, Mahan realized there was no formal coordination of these activities, and they were sometimes chaotic. Lieutenant Mahan suggested to Capt. Steve Waugh that the department needed a person to take charge of scheduling special events, making sure all necessary permits were obtained and sufficient personnel were assigned to properly run them. He further recommended that assigned officers work the details on an overtime basis, removing any doubt as to their status as law-enforcement officers and eliminating problems that could be caused by having to take orders from "civilian" bosses. Captain Waugh thought the idea had merit and brought it to the attention of Sheriff John McCarthy, who liked the idea, too. He liked it so much that he appointed Lt. Mahan as Metro's first Special Events Coordinator.

Mahan met many famous stars and sports personalities while carrying out his duties. He encountered some people of lesser character, too, however.

"I remember one Chinese movie company wanted to do a chase scene, ending with a crash in

**Dwight Mahan with
Nancy Reagan (above)
and Ronald Reagan (left)**

front of the Stardust. All clients had to pay the costs of our services up front, and when this outfit tried to pay with a check drawn on a foreign bank I refused to accept it. They were going to straighten things out and get right back to me; I never heard from them again.

Search and Rescue Unit—1986

"Some of the real low-budget people would try to get the shots they needed on their own. They'd walk around the inside of a casino with the camera running under their arm and hope nobody noticed it. They invariably got caught, but some of them still kept trying," he laughs.

Another part of Mahan's job was to coordinate security for visiting dignitaries. Working with the Secret Service, State Department, or foreign security services, he was responsible for the safety of presidents, vice presidents, first ladies, and foreign heads of state. "We never lost a guest," he grins.

In 1986, Lt. Mahan transferred to Air Support/Search and Rescue Services, where he served until his retirement.

"We supported the ground troops," Mahan said of the Air Support function. When he joined

the unit, it consisted of three helicopters and seven people. A crew of two, both qualified pilots and sworn officers, manned each chopper. When the helicopters weren't assisting their land-based colleagues handling crimes in progress or tracking fleeing suspects, they conducted routine patrol activities. Beginning under Lt. Mahan's leadership and continuing beyond, the Air Support program expanded. Although the mission has remained pretty much the same, in 2003 the operation had a fleet of four McDonnell Douglas MD 500s, two Bell HH-1H helicopters, and 16 pilots.

The Search and Rescue unit was founded in 1986, replacing the Sheriff's Jeep Posse. "The Jeep Posse consisted of one sergeant and one sworn officer; the rest were volunteers," Mahan recalls. "The trouble was, we were seeking accreditation from the Commission on Accreditation for Law Enforcement Agencies at the time and the way the Posse was set up wouldn't have met their criteria. Most of the volunteers had their private vehicles painted black and white and the majority of them carried guns. In addition to CALEA, those things created potential liability problems. And sometimes the volunteers would arrive on a scene and try to take charge of the operation away from sworn personnel. To address those concerns, I rewrote the Posse's bylaws, but they refused to accept them. They wanted to negotiate directly with Sheriff Moran. There was no negotiation and Moran abolished the Posse the next day. That's when the Search and Rescue unit came into being. Some of the former Posse volunteers joined the new unit, but certainly not all of them."

Today, Search and Rescue combines a permanent staff of seven sworn officers, supplemented by 50 unpaid civilian volunteers. A number of their calls involve assisting stranded mountain climbers, often at Red Rock Canyon. About 30 volunteers are assigned to the Mountain Rescue Team. These are people with special expertise as mountaineers, cavers, and rock climbers. Other volunteers have special skills, such as scuba divers, firefighters, paramedics, doctors, and nurses. Additional volunteer support teams consist of personnel experienced in handling search dogs and logistics.

The sworn officers are all medics and one or two participate in every SWAT operation. They have treated wounded or injured officers and suspects as well.

Search and Rescue receives more than 100 volunteer applications per year and performs about 100 rescues annually, many of which are life-saving efforts.

"It's one of the best Search and Rescue Teams in the United States today," Mahan says proudly of the unit he was instrumental in starting.

Career Cop

Lee McCullough was born in West Virginia and moved to Las Vegas in 1954. Working as a musician, he appeared in lounge acts in a variety of casinos. Growing dissatisfied with the irregular paychecks he was earning as an entertainer, he traded in his drums for the badge and gun of the Clark County Sheriff's Department in June 1957. Over the next 33 years, he was instrumental in implement-

ORIGINAL
LVMPD S.W.A.T. UNIT
ESTABLISHED JULY 4, 1976
RALPH LAMB SHERIFF

L. McCULLOUGH   E. COOPER

L. McDONNELL   R. TRAVERS   W. IKNER   D. MAHAN   T. MAURINE   R. McKEE

M. WYSOCKI   M. HAWKINS   J. FOX   R. SICILIANO   S. FRANKS   R. BOYCE

ing or improving many of the law-enforcement functions performed by his department. Captain McCullough retired from Metro in July 1990. During a February 2003 interview, he talked about his career.

"I liked the entertainment business, but you couldn't count on a steady income. I got to be friendly with some of the deputies who stopped in the casinos for their meals. I was talking to the guys one night and they told me the Sheriff's Department was putting on some more people. They suggested that I apply and see if they'd hire me. I did, and they did."

When McCullough first donned his uniform, Butch Leypoldt was his boss and the depart-ment had 36 sworn personnel. Headquarter was located in the county building on Third Street and the jail was in the basement.

"It was the best extradition jail in the country," according to McCullough. "Conditions were such that none of the prisoners fought against being extradited back to where they were wanted. They couldn't wait to get out of there."

He believes the merger be-tween the Clark County Sheriff's Department and the Las Vegas Police Department in 1973 was a good move, though fraught with difficulties for the first year. "There were hard feelings between some of the officers, professional jealousies and things like that. The deputies were considered better disciplined and the Las Vegas cops were more freewheeling. We didn't get the same uniforms and equipment for several months, and then things started to come around."

After the consolidation, Mc-Cullough, a lieutenant, became the supervisor of the Patrol Division's field-training officers. He was responsible for the continuing training of recruits after their graduation from the police academy and during their probationary period.

In 1976, he became the first commander of the newly formed Special Weapons and Tactics section. "I recall this aspect of my career with the greatest fondness. It isn't simply because I was selected as the first commander. SWAT was my baby; I was the primary driving force in convincing the department that creating the unit was logical and necessary in dealing with the increasing number of armed and violent confrontations officers were facing. It wasn't an easy sale," McCullough said.

In 1979 he moved on to become the Night Patrol Watch Commander. That was followed by a 1980 assignment as the South Area Patrol Commander.

A promotion to captain in 1981 resulted in another change of duty for McCullough, this time as Detective Bureau Commander. Then in 1983, he transferred to the job from which he would retire:

K-9 Officer training attack dog

SWAT cops in action

Special Operations Bureau Commander. He was responsible for the Traffic Division, SWAT and K-9 sections, Air Support, Search and Rescue, and the Resident Officer section.

Through promotion and transfer opportunities, Lee McCullough worked in, supervised, or commanded most of the sections in the Metropolitan Police Department. That placed him in a unique position to influence the development of the agency.

As an example, McCullough cites the K-9 section. "The K-9 program was a product of the LVPD that came to Metro after the merger; the dogs they had were donated by private citizens. For the most part they were animals people didn't want for one reason or another. They received inadequate training and were not totally reliable when called upon. In fact, some officers were reluctant to request a dog in situations where a K-9 response would have been appropriate. Some of the animals were fence-jumpers and biters that were apt to attack anybody around. At times, an innocent onlooker could be as much at risk from those dogs as the suspect. The street officers knew it and were understandably hesitant to ask for K-9 assistance.

"In order to correct the problems, we disbanded the K-9 operation and reorganized. For fourteen weeks Metro had no operational K-9 section. Sergeant Roy Stephenson put together a training program, the same program that's still used today. We got the money to buy top-quality purebred German Shepherds. We recruited, screened, and trained new officers who demonstrated proficiency in handling the dogs. It took a lot of effort, but when we were finished, we had a top-notch K-9 unit."

In addition, Lee McCullough developed and commanded the Hostage Negotiator Teams and the Street Crimes Attack Team.

One of the accomplishments of which he is the most proud involves the consolidation of police services that formed Metro: He designed the badge for the new agency. "It's nice to know that everybody out there is walking around with a little piece of me on them," he said.

McCullough is recognized in both Nevada and U.S. courts as a firearms and fingerprint expert. He's also a licensed private pilot.

After his retirement from Metro, he worked as a private security supervisor and a private investigator. He retired completely in 1999.

Female On Patrol

Georganne Lee moved to Las Vegas from Cincinnati, Ohio, in 1964. In 1965 she married Las Vegas Police Department Officer O. C. Lee. After seven years performing as a dancer, including stints with *Hello America* at the Desert Inn and *Casino De Paris* at the Dunes, she hired on with the Clark County Sheriff's Department in 1971. Her first assignment was as a meter maid at McCarran Airport. In 1973, she became one of the first women Metro assigned to street-patrol duty. In an April 2003 interview she recalled her days as a female Patrol officer.

"I have to say it was quite a change from dancing on the Strip to patrolling it. It all came about because Metro was under pressure to hire minorities at the time. They were receiving education grant money through the Law Enforcement Assistance Administration, but in order to keep on the program they had to hire females. Four women, including myself, were already on the payroll and had been through the academy. I was working at McCarran Airport as a meter maid and the other three were dispatchers. When it was decided to put females on the street, we were the first to be considered.

"We took the written tests, the physical agility, and the oral boards. There was a problem with the psychological test because it hadn't been rewritten and was designed with only male candidates in mind. There were questions like: Would you rather date a nurse or a waitress? Would you rather be an electrician or a plumber? When you go fishing, would you rather bait the hook or clean the fish? When hunting, do you prefer to shoot the animal or gut the kill?

"Getting fitted for a uniform was a challenge. As with the psychological test, the uniforms available were for men. Finding a pair of slacks small enough to fit was nearly impossible. When the seamstress tailored my pants, she had to alter them so much that the two rear pockets came together at the back seam.

Georganne Lee

"In addition to getting my pants to fit, my rather small waist created another problem: equipment storage. My gun belt didn't have an inch of room left after I was outfitted. It had to hold a holster, two magazine pouches, mace, handcuff case, flashlight, radio case, and nightstick ring. It was impossible to get in a comfortable position sitting in the patrol car. Going to the restroom in a gas station was really something. The belt had to be taken completely off and you didn't want to put it on the floor for fear somebody would reach under the stall door and grab it while you were unable to give pursuit. Since there was usually no other place to hang it, I draped it around my neck. Then there was the impact that seeing a pair of boots on the floor of the stall, or hearing the police radio, had on other females wanting to use the facilities. They frequently assumed that a man had gotten into the ladies room and would flee to find a manager or call the police. I seriously curtailed my coffee drinking while on duty."

Aside from these difficulties, how about performing actual police duties and dealing with the public?

"The women were ready for the streets, but were the streets ready for us? No, they weren't. Not only was the public slow to accept female officers working in Patrol, so were the wives of our male colleagues. Many spouses didn't think a female would be there for the men if things got tough. In reality, it was often the other way around. The men wanted us to prove ourselves and would sometimes hang back to see how we handled various situations. I think that women are protective by nature and we fiercely defended our male partners.

"As for the public, we weren't overnight successes with them either. Their reactions when a woman officer responded to a call ranged from disbelief to anger. I remember going to a prowler call and the homeowner, a big husky guy, wasn't the least bit happy with me. 'I called for a cop, not a damned woman. If I'd known they were going to send a female, I'd have checked out the backyard myself. I don't need any woman looking out for me, so you can just get the hell out of here,' he hollered. Then he slammed the door in my face.

"On the other hand, being a female officer when responding to a bar fight sometimes brought the action to a quick conclusion, but not because the combatants were intimidated. They'd break out laughing at the thought of a girl subduing five or six brawlers. You'd hear comments like: 'You've got to be kidding me.' Or, 'Is this some kind of a joke?' One guy wanted to know if we were staging a stunt for 'Candid Camera.'

"Sometimes we'd scare the guys, though. We weren't physically threatening, but they couldn't be sure how we'd react if they didn't obey our commands. Since they probably figured we weren't capable of restraining them with our hands, maybe we'd just shoot them. Those possibilities kept them guessing until the novelty of female cops wore off.

"I was bitten twice, once by a roller-derby queen and once by a drug addict. The girl butted me in the head, and then aimed her mouth at my chest. I turned before her teeth found their target and she bit my shoulder instead. The addict got me on the arm and I had to go to the hospital for shots. The next day I read in the paper: 'Turn of events—suspect puts bite on cop.' I guess it was quite an entertaining story.

"It was good that women finally started working the street, though. There were certain situations that we were better equipped to handle than the men. For example, a rape victim was usually much more comfortable dealing with a female cop.

"After a while my priorities started to change. I realized there was more to life than chasing suspects, arresting drug addicts, and responding to a beaten child or suicide call. I found myself getting frustrated with the criminal-justice system and hearing too many 'not-guilty' verdicts. It seemed that sometimes you were the enemy of the criminal element and the system as well. Disenchanted, I got out of Patrol in 1976 and went back to my former job at the airport. Later, I went to work for Clark County as an operations coordinator, handling emergency landings, bomb threats, plane crashes, and hijackings. I was a liaison between Metro, the FAA, the Fire Department, and Civil Defense.

"Late one evening in March 1980, two somber-looking officers knocked on my door and told me that my husband had been shot in the head. He was alive, but in critical condition. I went to the hospital and learned that part of the bullet had exited his ear and the rest was lodged in the back of his head, just missing the spinal column. After three months recuperating at home, he went back to work with the bullet still in him. He knew he'd never be able to work the street again and desk duty was driving him nuts. He had always been active in the police union and ran for election as its president. He won and that became his full-time job. He eventually had several successful surgeries, including one to remove the bullet from his head.

"In 1991, the Police Protective Association voted to change the name of their building to the O. C. Lee Building in gratitude for all he had done to benefit police officers throughout the years. The week that initiative was announced, I received several unnerving phone calls expressing condolences over my husband's death. It seemed that people thought a building could only be named for a specific individual after that person was deceased. I was pleased to be able to inform the callers that wasn't the case.

"As for me, I'm glad I had the opportunity to blaze the trail for other female officers to follow. It was an experience that taught me a great deal about loyalties and human nature. While working for Clark County, I returned to college and obtained my degree in psychology. In 1985, I opened my own business, Motivation Unlimited, and ran it for eight years."

After the couple retired in 1992, O.C. Lee became a state senator and Georganne pursued her many hobbies. Today, they travel extensively and enjoy life to the fullest.

Undersheriff

Eric Cooper was born in Cincinnati, Ohio, in 1940. He moved to Las Vegas with his family in 1950. After graduating from Las Vegas High School in 1958, he joined the Marine Corps. During his four-year enlistment, he was stationed at a number of posts, including the Philippines and Japan. Cooper started with the Reserve Program of the Las Vegas Police Department in 1963 and became a regular officer the following year. After Metro was formed in 1973, he rose through the ranks and attained the position of Chief of Detectives. In January 1983, he was selected by incoming Sheriff John Moran to serve as his Undersheriff.

Eric Cooper

In an interview in March 2003, Undersheriff Cooper recalled his 12 years occupying Metro's second spot.

"The Moran administration came into office after four very controversial years under Sheriff John McCarthy. Sheriff Moran had made several campaign pledges that would address major issues confronting the Valley. One of them had to do with getting the prostitution problem under control. It had gotten to the point where tourists or law-abiding locals couldn't walk the Strip without being accosted by a hooker. Moran promised to resolve that issue within the first ninety days of his term, and we did.

"In addition to that, we were facing increasing gang crime in general, and the Cuban Marielitos were becoming a real problem. We had our work cut out for us, but we hit the ground running and did what needed to be done. The effective way in which we handled the Marielitos served as a model for other police agencies across the country.

"Another area we had to confront was the low morale that existed. During the previous four years the department had been in such a state of turmoil that it wasn't as effective as it might have been. When we took office we encouraged risk-taking and innovative thinking and got away from the 'zero defects' style of administration typical of many police departments. We knew we needed to take steps to restore the self-esteem of our officers and get the agency moving forward again. One of the things we wanted to do was be recognized as a top-of-the-line police department by getting national accreditation. The idea was good, but implementing it was easier said than done."

Why was that?

"Metro was not very highly regarded by other agencies. We had the 'Sin City' image and had recently come through a scandal regarding some officers providing information to organized-crime figures. The International Association of Chiefs of Police even questioned the wisdom of having their convention in Las Vegas. They were concerned that the association with our city might tarnish their reputation. I was determined to get the word out that Metro did not fit that perception. We were not a corrupt department. Like any large department, we had our rogues, but we rooted them out and dealt with them.

"We applied to CALEA, the Commission on Accreditation for Law Enforcement Agencies. In order to be accredited, you have to meet a number of standards. Accreditation by CALEA is not automatic; it's a long and tough process. In July 1989, we received our first accreditation. Metro became the 112th agency so accredited nationwide and the first in Nevada. Besides our efforts for national recognition, we began awarding officers for exemplary performance. Some of the award winners have been featured in *Parade* and *International Association of Chiefs of Police* magazines. In other words, the awards were prestigious and meant something to the recipients. I truly believe these actions are greatly responsible for elevating Metro to the status of its current reputation," Cooper said proudly.

Since the initial accreditation in 1989, Metro was re-accredited in 1994 and 1999. The department received its first three-year accreditation in 2002 and is scheduled for on-site accreditation in 2005. For an agency of Metro's size, CALEA has 442 standards, not all of which are mandatory. Metro complied with 437 of them.

Metro is one of only 19 police agencies in the United States and Canada to be accredited through all three of the law-enforcement accrediting agencies: CALEA, the National Commission on Correctional Health, and the American Correctional Association.

"Over time we did many other things to improve both the perception and the actual operation of the department," Cooper continued. "For example, our ranking in the FBI's Uniform Crime Reports for serious crimes was dismal, in the top two or three worst in the country when Moran took over. We tackled the problem aggressively and those rankings began to drop rapidly. By Moran's second term we were all the way down to around 150th. I'm sure that trend continues today. Another program we instituted was allowing officers to carry alternate weapons. The logic was that some people are more comfortable with one weapon than another. As such, they are likely to be more accurate and confident with their preferred handgun. The 9mm was the standard department sidearm, but we gave our people the option of carrying a 10mm, 40 or 45 caliber semi-automatic, or a .357 revolver with a six-inch barrel. There was one argument against it: If all officers used the same guns, they could share ammunition in an emergency. We checked and couldn't find a police department anywhere in the country where officers had to share ammo in an actual shooting situation. Metro was the first agency in the country to allow alternate weapons and it was very popular with the troops.

"These were all things that helped to modernize the department and move it forward. That modernization has continued, but

I believe that our administration set the tone. We got the ball rolling and those that followed kept it going."

There were many positives, but there must have been some negatives, too. What were the major disappointments?

"I'd have to say there were three things that bothered me the most. The first was when a guy died after a scuffle with Vice Detectives in his apartment. His girlfriend had just been arrested on the street for prostitution and the detectives were doing a follow-up investigation to determine if the boyfriend, Charles Bush, was acting as her pimp. After an investigation, all three of the detectives involved were charged criminally with Involuntary Manslaughter and Oppression Under the Color of Law. They were subsequently acquitted, but the case dragged on for quite a while and the department took a bad beating in the press. Those are not among my fondest memories.

"The second thing was when some of our minority officers filed a federal discrimination lawsuit against the department. I read their allegations and couldn't believe all that they were saying. That was another situation that lingered on and received quite a bit of adverse press attention. It was a pain in the neck for a while, but I applauded the consent decree when it was signed, because it did correct some deficiencies. In fact, I ended up becoming a cheerleader for it.

"Third were the Rodney King riots. They lasted for weeks and really put the department to the test.

"If I had to give a reason why I was ready to move on to other things when Sheriff Moran decided not to seek a fourth term, the Bush death and the King riots would be part of it. The other thing was the process of running for office. I guess I can say I love police work, but I hate politics.

"Those things aside, I'm very proud of my tenure as Undersheriff and what the Moran administration accomplished. I think we can claim a lot of the credit for shaping Metro into the first-class operation it is today."

In 1994, John Moran declined to seek another term. Eric Cooper left Metro when Jerry Keller took office in January 1995. After retiring, he spent six years as a Reserve Deputy Sheriff in Douglas County, Nevada. He also acted as a lobbyist for the Nevada Sheriffs and Chiefs Association. He is currently a part-time hearing officer for the Nevada Board of Parole Commissioners. He is a licensed pilot and enjoys competitive shooting.

The Recruit

Nina Radetich is co-anchor of the afternoon and night newscasts on Channel 3, KVBC-TV in Las Vegas. The native Californian began her television career with KAB in Los Angeles in 1994. After a time at KERO-TV in Bakersfield, she moved to Las Vegas in 1996 and joined KVBC as a weekend morning anchor. Her Crime Tracker 3 segment has garnered several awards, including Electronic Media awards for best regularly scheduled feature and a Jerry Lee Foundation award recognizing effective crime-prevention programming.

Nina Radetich

In July 2000, Nina's efforts to experience what police officers must go through to earn their badges paid off. She was permitted to attend the Las Vegas Metropolitan Police Department's training academy class 3-2000. The agreement between Channel 3 and Metro provided for her to attend three weeks of the 21-week class. She would be subject to the same treatment and discipline as her classmates. Nina's series of reports on her academy experiences earned an Edward R. Murrow award for journalistic excellence. In April 2003, she reflected on those three weeks.

"I ended up as a recruit at the police academy because I wanted to get the most unconventional in-depth look possible at how Metro officers earn their badges. Attending the Citizen's Academy or interviewing staff wouldn't be enough. A couple of days observing in the classroom wouldn't tell the whole story. I determined that in order to give viewers a true glimpse of police work at its root, I had to become a recruit and go through what they go through," she said.

"I made the necessary requests and contacts to set everything up. As I ran the idea by more and more people, it seemed that a lot of them were smirking. I wondered what was the big deal. I'd always wanted to go through some type of boot camp. I was physically fit and mentally strong, and didn't think it would be that difficult for me.

"Like everyone else, I started out with the testing process, physical first. Running and sit-ups were no problem. Then came a reality check: I couldn't do any pushups, and pushups are a basic academy requirement. The Metro higher-ups allowed me to pass anyway, but I knew if I didn't get a grip on those pushups, I'd be in for it during the academy.

"Next was the written test; I scored an eighty-eight percent. The oral boards followed. It was no fun sitting in a room with three police officers who show no emotion and give zero feedback to your responses. I found that reacting to an imaginary situation on tape is incredibly awkward. I begged off on the background check and psychological examination, figuring Metro didn't need to know my deepest darkest secrets. I understood the basic premise, though: The screening process is intense; you don't just apply to be a cop and then start cop school.

"After all the preliminary stuff was out of the way, it was time to focus on the academy itself. I got fitted for a uniform, bought some boots, and stocked up on the recommended necessities. As the start date grew closer, I began to understand what I was really in for. Case in point: payroll-processing day. I was late, of course, a bad habit

broken thanks to the academy. Two training academy Tactical (TAC) officers met me at the door and gave me a good going-over, almost invoking tears they scared me so much. I believe the words were: 'Ma'am, tardiness will not be tolerated in this academy. Discipline will follow should you choose to be late again.' It wasn't the words, but the tone in which they were delivered that made them scary. Some had wondered if I'd receive special treatment. The question was put to rest that day.

"Orientation week didn't start off too bad; the TAC officers were actually friendly at the beginning. We covered inspection procedures, got familiar with our gun belts, and went through a basic introduction to firearms. By the end of the week, playtime was over, though. We had a debriefing and were then given five minutes to clear the building and assemble in a park across the street to practice military facing movements. Chaos ensued as we tried to clear out. I got chased down the hall with a TAC officer screaming in my face. I'd never been so intimidated or fearful in my life. When we were dismissed an hour later, I got in my car and cried all the way home.

"Two days later we had the dreaded first inspection. As a class, we'd gotten together on our days off and gone over the drill, relying heavily on recruits with prior military experience. As we waited, I wondered if I'd be able to do the pushups if we were punished. I'd been practicing and hoped I'd be able to handle it if I had to.

"When I presented my gun for inspection, my hand was sweating so badly I was afraid the firearm would slip out and fall to the ground. I answered the questions thrown at me about codes and definitions with relative ease. As a class, we had to do a lot of running and pushups that day, how many I can't guess. I only know that it was the longest hour and a half of my life. Still, after it was over I felt stronger. Getting through that first inspection is a major milestone at the academy. I assumed it could only get better.

"I'd always considered time management my strong suit. Even so, after ten hours in the classroom, the last thing I wanted to do was study, polish my boots, and get my uniform ready for the next day. I felt fortunate to be a single woman, with only myself to worry about. Several of my classmates had wives, husbands and small children at home. I marveled at their ability to cope.

"I got accustomed to what was expected of me, spending two or three hours every night hitting the books and studying flash cards. I also talked on the phone with mem-bers of the class. It felt good to be part of a growing team and we were all in it together. The difference was, I only had three weeks and I'd be through. The others had a long road still ahead of them to become law-enforcement officers.

"Those three weeks at the academy provided just enough for an overview: one written test, some defensive tactics, a fitness test, and what seemed like years of class-room instruction. Our first day of physical training caused me to ask myself a question: Can you really work out for seven hours straight? Apparently in police work, you can. It's amazing how much you can do with someone yelling at you to perform. I learned that your body is only limited by your mind, a realization that has stuck with me since the academy. In spite of the soreness after those seven hours, I passed the test with no problem. I did thirty pushups in a minute; prior to the academy I was lucky if I could do two.

"Inspiration, motivation, and a whole new perspective—that's what my time as a recruit gave me. I walked in only expecting that attending the academy would be fun, and a unique way to get a story that would be of interest to the Las Vegas community. What I didn't realize was that I'd walk away with personal benefits. I credit the acad-emy with strengthening my drive, both personally and professionally. I credit the academy with opening my eyes to not only what police officers have to endure, but to what any person can endure if they have the will. Finally, I credit the academy with making me a stronger and more confident individual, who understands the importance of teamwork."

After the academy, it took Nina two months to put together a five-part series about police training in Las Vegas. She considers that project to be the best work of her television career.

The Accident

Russ Peterson

Officer Russ Peterson was hired by Metro in April 1990. In 1996, he was assigned to the Search and Rescue Unit. This duty allowed him to combine a love of the outdoors with his law-enforcement career. The next two years would be the happiest of his professional life. In March 1998, a tragic training accident claimed Officer Peterson's life. In a January 2003 interview, his widow, Lesa Peterson, remembered her husband and the day that changed her life.

"We met in 1983 in our home town of Kankakee, Illinois. Russ was a tae kwon do instructor and I was one of his students. He wasn't in it for the money. He only charged the students enough to cover the cost of renting the building; that was the way Russ was. Anyway, we started dating and were engaged nine months later. We got married on April 6, 1985. Two days later we left for Provo, Utah, where Russ had the promise of a job in the police department there. Three months later he was working as a patrolman. Within a year I was hired as a corrections officer by the Utah County Sheriff's Department.

"We both loved the outdoors and before long we were doing lots of hiking and backpacking. Another officer got Russ and me interested in rock climbing, and it was something we really liked right from the start. He was very active in the department and was especially interested in firearms training, officer safety, and search-and-rescue operations. In the five years we were in Provo, he served as a firearms instructor and on the Special Response Team, a SWAT equivalent. He was involved with the new Search and Rescue Team. Russ loved his work, but he began looking for a bigger department where there would be more opportunity.

"In early 1990 he found Metro and we moved to Las Vegas. He scored number one in the testing process and was hired that April. Six years later he got assigned to Search and Rescue. For the next two years I can't imagine that he could have been any happier. Russ had turned forty on March 23, 1998, and we celebrated his birthday. And then the next day, everything changed.

"Russ was very excited because of new climbing techniques he had learned at a seminar in Colorado the previous week. That morning he and one of the Search and Rescue volunteers went to Mt. Charleston to practice climb. I went about my daily routine, going to work at the Monte Carlo Hotel and then on to the Community College, where I was taking human anatomy and physiology courses.

"I got home from school around seven-thirty that night. About a half an hour later there was a knock at my door. When I opened it, I found Sergeant Tom Harmon of PEAP, Sheriff Keller and his wife, Bill Cassell, who was partnered with Russ, and his wife, Nancy, standing there. I knew right away that something bad had happened, but I had no idea of the magnitude. I thought they were going to tell me Russ had been injured and was in the hospital. When everyone was inside, Tom told me that Russ had been killed. At that point they weren't sure of the details, but thought he had fallen during the climb. I had a hard time accepting that explanation, because Russ was always so careful. I couldn't imagine him being careless and that really bothered me. As more information became available, I learned that Russ died as the result of an avalanche and had done nothing wrong that contributed to his death. It may not make any sense, but at the time that made me feel better.

"Over the next several hours the facts surrounding my husband's death became clearer. Russ and his climbing partner, Jim, were nearly finished for the day. They were descending the ice when a freak avalanche roared down on them. Russ was below Jim, steadying the rope. Large chunks of ice hurtled down just missing Jim's head, but hitting

Russ. It was later determined that one of the projectiles that struck him broke his neck, and he died instantly. Jim survived a second avalanche before making it to the ground and calling for help.

"Early the next morning Bill and Nancy picked me up and took me to the mountain. The team finally arrived where we were waiting, carrying Russ on a litter. The team members formed a circle around the litter to block out the media cameras. Two of the officers unzipped the body bag and I was finally able to see him. He looked peaceful, like he was sleeping. He didn't appear injured; his glasses were on and there wasn't a scratch on them. This, too, provided a degree of comfort and closure.

"After the coroner removed the body, we all went to the Search and Rescue headquarters for a debriefing. Everyone there shared whatever feelings they felt were appropriate. I had never been involved with anything like that before, and found it to be a very emotional and healing experience.

"I received tremendous support from Metro during the ordeal. Bill Young and Sergeant Harmon were particularly helpful in making arrangements and assuring that everything went smoothly. I could not have asked any more of the department than what they willingly gave me. Quite frankly, I don't know what I'd have done without them."

Three months after her husband was killed, Metro hired Lesa Peterson as a Crime Scene Analyst. She worked in that position for 14 months before returning to college. She also worked as a firearms instructor, providing the required training to persons seeking permits to carry concealed weapons in Clark County. Lesa received her B.A. in May 2003.

Keller Years

Richard Winget was born in Panguitch, Utah, and moved with his family to Las Vegas at the age of four. He began his career with the Clark County Sheriff's Department in 1973, just prior to the consolidation with the Las Vegas Police Department that formed Metro. He enjoyed a steady rise through the ranks and was promoted to deputy chief in 1991. Sheriff Jerry Keller tapped Winget to be his second-in-command when he assumed office in January 1995.

In an October 23, 2002, interview, I asked Undersheriff Winget if there were any particular accomplishments of the Keller administration he wanted to mention. He provided me with a copy of a document he had prepared a couple of weeks earlier called "That of Which I am Most Proud." He explained that it was a record reflecting his eight years serving under Sheriff Keller and would be used as the basis for a future article in Metro's *Training Wheel* magazine.

In May 2002, Nevada Senator John Ensign recommended Undersheriff Winget as United States Marshal, District of Nevada. President George W. Bush appointed him to that position on March 31, 2003.

"That of Which I am Most Proud"
by Richard Winget

Recently I was watching a debate between two general election candidates for District Attorney. Jon Ralston asked a very interesting question of Assistant District Attorney Michael Davidson. He asked, "In your four and a half years with the District Attorney's office, describe that of which you are most proud." What a great question! The more I thought, the more I realized how much we have accomplished, and I decided to make that question the topic of my farewell message to the men and women of the Las Vegas Metropolitan Police Department. Following is a discussion of that of which I am most proud our last eight years. Before I begin, it must be clear that these are not things that I personally accomplished, but those that we as an organization accomplished. Credit must be spread wide and far, and we can all stand proud for what we have done and where we are going.

Over the last seven years we have dramatically impacted the crime rate in our community. Violent crime is down 42%; property crimes are down 38%; and overall, the crime rate has dropped by 39%. All this while our service population grew by 38%. Crime rate is a ruler by which we as a police department are often judged, and again, we can stand proud.

In the last eight years we have added 848 police officers to the streets of Las Vegas and 50 corrections officers to the decks of the jail. At the same time, we added 658 support personnel, so important for the smooth operation of our police department. They have been added to Communications, Criminalistics, Police and Detention Records, Evidence Vault, Area Commands and throughout the organization. We established ratios of two officers per 100,000 residents and one support person for every two police officers. These ratios have provided guidance in establishing budgets and given credibility to our requests of the City and County for additional personnel. We have not only added personnel, but we have added a system to ensure that future personnel needs will be identified and justified.

In 1998/99 our jurisdiction was plagued with meth labs and meth dealers. In that year, we disassembled 427 labs in our community. We established street narcotics teams and trained crime scene investigators to deal with these toxic scenes, coordinated activities with Patrol and worked with the legislature to curtail pre-cursor drugs. This year, to date, we have had only 120 labs.

I realize that we cannot make our community safe simply by throwing people in jail, for we cannot build enough jails nor build enough prisons. We, as a police department, must be part of a community-wide effort to deal with the underlying issues that cause criminal activity. In this arena, I am most proud of our department's establishment of the first police athletic league (PAL) in Clark County. PAL officers provide hope to at-risk youth who see no hope. PAL provides opportunities for athletic competitions, tutoring, coaching and mentoring.

I am proud of the supervisors and officers who have worked so hard to make this unit effective.

I am proud of our organization's awards of accreditation. We received our first award through CALEA under Sheriff Moran's leadership. Subsequently, we have been accredited four times, and have added accreditations of our corrections operations through the Commission on Accreditation for Corrections and our correctional healthcare through the National Commission on Correctional Healthcare. This culminated with the Triple Crown Award being issued by the National Sheriff's Association in 1998. This is a very prestigious award that documents excellence in police, corrections and correctional healthcare. It has been awarded to only 16 agencies internationally. We were the 10th.

For decades, one of the problems that plagued us as an organization most significantly has been a lack of space in which to work. Working with the City of Las Vegas, we added the Downtown Area Command; working with Clark County, we added the South Central Area Command; and working with both the City and County, we added the Bolden Area Command. In addition, we built a new Northwest Area Command, Southeast Area Command, Training Center, and Communications Center and have begun construction on a new Fingerprint building and a new Fleet building. We have obtained the property and begun the planning for a new Police Headquarters Building to be built near the Clark County Government Center and Regional Transportation Center. During this fiscal year, we will do the space planning; next year we will develop the architectural plans; and in the years that follow, the Police Headquarters Building will become a reality.

In 1994, considerable unrest existed in our organization because of a conceived inconsistency of discipline. Since that time, we have established the Labor Relations Unit and developed a discipline matrix, both of which have come a long way to ensuring that an employee in Patrol who commits a similar offense under similar circumstances as another employee in Intelligence will receive similar discipline. While the system is not perfect, we have come a long way. More work has to be done, but I am proud of what we have accomplished.

I am proud of our strategic planning process. From a system that originally simply filled a book, we now enjoy a system that has become the backbone of our planning, budgeting and operations. I don't believe there is an employee in our organization who can't identify our fundamental values and discuss how they guide our actions and conduct. I am confident that every supervisor and cop in our organization can develop tactical plans and understands how they support our strategies and goals. Our vision of becoming the best law enforcement agency in partnership with our community has become a reality.

I am proud of our lateral-entry program and our mounted unit. Both were developed during the past eight years; both have made their mark on our organization; both have proved their worth.

I am proud of our leadership-training program. We are committed to developing our leaders. The program includes personalized development plans, systems for identifying strengths and weaknesses and a long-term plan for continual growth. We just started our second class and participants are enthusiastic about their future.

In short, I am proud of the men and women of the Las Vegas Metropolitan Police Department. I am proud of what you do, how you act, who you are and where you are going. I will always hold my head high when my name is linked to this police department. The issues discussed in this article are but a few of the reasons why you should all do the same. Thank you for 30 great years. You are the best.

Appendix A

LVMPD
Medal of Honor Recipients

    This commendation is awarded to a member for a distinctive act that extends above and beyond the normal call of duty, or service performed at a risk to personal safety or life in an effort to protect property or save human life.

Recipient	Incident Date	Synopsis
John Edwards	6/14/76	This officer entered a gas-filled trailer to rescue a three-year-old girl.
Robert Griffith Marc Kahre	10/29/76	Awarded for acts of heroism while responding to an apartment fire.
Larry Sigglekow	10/27/78	Awarded for exemplary conduct while responding to a plane crash.
Ray Flynn	2/10/82	Fired at suspect who was holding a gun on another officer.
Brenda Boyce Larry Mosser	8/7/85	For actions while attempting to save a 17-month-old baby from a fire.
Danny Harness	4/12/91	Saved six people from a burning building.

Recipient	Incident Date	Synopsis
David Devito	4/2/94	Captured a bank robber while off-duty.
Csaba Maczala	10/3/94	Saved two people from a burning building.
Merl Sage	3/21/95	While off-duty, rescued a woman who was being sexually assaulted.
Charles Jones	12/22/95	While off-duty, intervened in an in-progress sexual assault. Officer Jones sustained physical injuries during the altercation.
John Faulis Donald Cullison	3/21/96	Entered a burning building six times attempting to save a couple who had been involved in a violent domestic situation in which shots were fired.
Jim Dixon	6/30/96	Awarded for actions when responding to a fire while off-duty.
Alexis Jackson	7/27/96	While in Atlanta, Georgia, Officer Jackson assisted victims of the Olympic Park bombing.
Dennis Durfey	10/7/96	Awarded for actions while in pursuit of a homicide suspect.
Luis Norris	1/28/97	Officer Norris was shot and wounded while responding to a family-disturbance call.
David Winslow Jeff Hodgkinson David Schvaneveldt	12/9/97	Rescued an elderly resident from a burning apartment.

Recipient	Incident Date	Synopsis
Stephen Hammack	12/9/97	Awarded for actions while engaging a vehicle pursuit in which shots were fired and the officer was wounded.
Gary Marsh Ralph Burton	9/8/98	Rescued two women from a vehicle trapped in rising flood waters.
Grant Graan Salvatore Mascoli Robert Schmidt Darren Heiner Joseph Pannullo	11/10/98	Awarded for actions after responding to a plant where an employee had destroyed several vehicles and killed his supervisor.
Collin Jotz Dominick Kaserkie	3/1/99	Officer Kaserkie was shot twice by an armed suspect who then jumped on the hood of the patrol car. Kaserkie swerved the vehicle and dislodged the subject. Officer Jotz, in a separate car, used his vehicle to pin the suspect and then administered aid to Officer Kaserkie.
William Schmitt	7/6/99	Rescued an individual from raging flood waters.
Kenneth Rios	8/20/99	While off-duty, saved an individual from a burning airplane.
Carlos Acosta Damian Walburn Charles Whitney Eric Collins Antonio Morales Timothy Gross Richard Barela	4/23/02	Awarded for actions during a hostage situation, while attempting to arrest an armed murder suspect.

Appendix B

LVMPD
Medal of Valor Recipients

This commendation is awarded to a member for an extraordinary act of heroism that extends far above and beyond the normal call of duty or service and is performed at great risk to personal safety in an effort to save human life.

Recipient	Incident Date	Synopsis
James Rogan	2/22/78	Officer Rogan was fatally shot during a traffic stop. His assailant was located the next day and was killed when he refused to surrender.
James Harbin	2/18/79	Corrections Officer Harbin was shot and killed when he entered a convenience store during an armed robbery. He was in uniform and on his way to work at the time.
Dave Morelli George Mantooth	8/8/80	Awarded for rescuing juveniles from a burning vehicle.
Tom Mildren Harry Christopher	11/21/80	Awarded for actions while operating an LVMPD helicopter during the MGM Hotel fire.

Recipient	Incident Date	Synopsis
Dan Mahony Glenn Thomas	10/12/81	Saved three people from a burning building.
Mike Horn Bob Roshak Mike Crason	3/7/82	Pulled two occupants from a burning vehicle.
Dan Purdy Bob Murray	7/10/84	Rescued occupants of a burning vehicle.
James Hulsey	10/11/88	Awarded for his efforts to protect Officer Marc Kahre from an assailant. Officer Kahre was shot and killed during the incident.
Rory Tuggle	4/30/92	Awarded for saving a man's life and leadership exhibited during the Rodney King riots.
Andrew Ramos	4/30/92	Saved a man's life during Rodney King riots.
Michael Brambila	5/20/94	After sustaining a gunshot wound, chased and captured a suspect.
Robert Manzer	5/26/94	Pursued two robbery suspects from a K-Mart parking lot after being shot.
Richard Servoss	2/24/97	Made multiple difficult helicopter landings on a mountaintop during a rescue and evacuated the victims to the trauma center.

Recipient	Incident Date	Synopsis
Andrew Patzer Edwin Serrano	2/26/97	Rescued occupants from a blazing apartment.
Dennis Devitte	12/5/99	While off-duty, engaged in a gun fight with armed robbers. During the melee, Officer Devitte fatally wounded one of the suspects while suffering eight gunshot wounds himself.
Michael Springer Jim Boubon	11/16/00	Officers were off-duty and at Springer's home when two masked gunmen entered. During the ensuing struggle both gunmen were shot and wounded.
Keith Borders	8/23/01	Responding to a domestic call, the officer made contact with the female victim in front of the residence. While interviewing her, the male emerged firing a shotgun. Officer Borders sustained a head wound while attempting to assure the safety of the female.
Carmen Donegan Mathew McCarthy Michael McNamee John Bradshaw Jim Dixon David Martel Stephen Novier Mathew Ruiz Jon Word Thomas Bachman	4/26/02	Officers responded to an apartment where they observed a broken window. The damage appeared to have been caused by a gunshot. With their knocks unanswered, the officers entered the apartment to check on the status of any occupants. A suspect opened fire with an AR-15, wounding Officers McCarthy and McNamee.

Recipient	Incident Date	Synopsis
Gary Hood Craig Olson	4/27/02	During the annual Laughlin River Run a violent event occurred at Harrah's Hotel. While pulling into Harrah's parking lot, approximately thirty-five members of the Hells Angels motorcycle gang drove past Hood's marked patrol car, parked their bikes, and ran inside. Knowing that a rival gang was already inside, Hood called for additional units and then he and Officer Olson entered the building. A fight was in progress and shots were being fired. After firing one shot at the bikers, the officers ordered everyone to the floor and controlled the mob until more personnel arrived.

Appendix C

Other Noteworthy LVMPD Programs and Projects

Year	Program/Project
1980	The Neighborhood Watch program was launched when 3,500 single-dwelling homes were formed into Neighborhood Watch groups. As a result of the program's rapid growth, Block Captains meetings were begun in 1984.
1983	The Special Trust Investigative Fund (Operation STIF) was implemented. It targeted the habitual or career criminal as well as those involved in organized-crime activities. When the first phase of STIF ended in October 1984, 134 suspects were arrested on state and federal felony charges. There were another 132 residual arrests. STIF II (Operation Chutzpah) targeted street crime offenders. It culminated in July 1985 with 24 arrests.
1984	STIF III (Operation Bastille), again targeting career criminals, ended in October 1985, with the arrests of 156 persons representing 463 felony counts.

The Mobile Home Protection Plan expanded the Neighborhood Watch concept to mobile-home parks. Unlike the original program, which involved only residents, the new initiative included the owners, managers, and tenants of mobile-home parks.

The Street Crime Attack Team (SCAT) was formed to combat specific crimes in specific areas. When the unit was dissolved, many of its members were absorbed by SWAT.

The Gang Diversion Unit was formed to combat growing

gang activity and their involvement in drug sales. The unit was instrumental in identifying the makeup and characteristics of the various gangs and used that information to educate other officers.

The unit also developed a "dealer impersonation" plan, which was used in several large operations, resulting in hundreds of arrests of both drug sellers and buyers. In 1989 the Gang Diversion Unit was transferred to the Selective Enforcement Bureau.

1985   Burglary Attack Teams (BAT) were created to address growing burglary problems. The teams were assigned to area stations and focused their efforts on apprehending known career criminals. As gang problems escalated, the teams were removed from the stations and renamed the Special Enforcement Detail. In 1989 they joined the Gang Diversion Unit in the Selective Enforcement Bureau.

The Crime Alert Telecomputing System (CAT) linked the security forces of the Las Vegas casinos and resorts with each other and the LVMPD. The system allowed crimes committed at those facilities to be reported to all other properties and the police within minutes. All costs associated with the system were funded by the resort and casino industry.

In August, the Secret Witness Crime Watch was introduced. The Community Relations Bureau and local television stations joined in producing and airing real-life reenactments of unsolved crimes. Broadcast on a weekly basis, the reenactments were filmed by the VMPD Audio Visual Unit and distributed to the television stations.

1986   The Street Narcotics Detail became operational in January. Targeting street level drug dealers and their suppliers, the unit made 119 arrests in its first month. Additionally, they seized 25 guns, 17 vehicles, and $90,606 in cash. During the first six months over 1,000 felons were arrested, 100 vehicles were seized, and $350,000 in drug money was impounded.

The Drug Abuse Resistance Education (DARE) Program was implemented. The initiative targeted elementary school students and featured officers from the Community Relations

Bureau dealing with the children in their school environment. The program was designed to instill self-esteem, communications skills, and positive alternatives to drug-abuse behavior.

In November, the 9-1-1 Emergency Telephone System was made available in the entire Las Vegas Valley. Calls for all emergency services were handled by the 9-1-1 Communications Center. A special feature of the enhanced system displayed the caller's address and phone number on a computer screen, allowing units to be dispatched even if the reporting person was unable to remain on the line to provide information.

1989   Line Solution Policing was introduced. Located at each of the area commands, teams were tasked with helping citizens resolve non-criminal problems. Those problems included decay and disorder and regaining control of neighborhoods. LSP officers coordinated problem resolution with patrol officers and other governmental agencies as appropriate. The citizens were kept engaged in the process through mailings, door-to-door surveys, and face-to-face meetings.

1991   April saw the implementation of the Use of Force Review Board. Designed to allow the Department and the community to examine use-of-force incidents involving officers, the Board is comprised of both sworn personnel and citizens who have applied to serve as members.

The first class of the Citizen Academy was held. Classes are held one night per week and the students learn about the LVMPD. Subjects are taught by sworn officers and include LVMPD organization, patrol and investigative procedures, a tour of the Clark County Correctional Facility, working a shift at the 9-1-1 Communications Center, and a ride along with a patrol officer.

Appendix D

LVMPD
Organizational Chart
effective January 6, 2003

Office of the Sheriff
Sheriff Bill Young
229-3231

Legal Affairs
Chief Kathryn Landreth
229-3304

Intergovernment Services
Lt. Stan Olsen
229-5538

Office of the Undersheriff
Undersheriff Doug Gillespie
229-3438

Finance Exec. Director
Karen Keller
229-1365

Public Information Office
Director Carla Alston
229-3394

Law Enforcement Services
Assistant Sheriff Ray Flynn
229-3438

Technical Services Division
Deputy Chief Dennis Cobb
229-3503

Communications Bureau
Capt. Mark Medina
229-3870

Records Bureau
Director Tracy Lang
229-3274

Fingerprint Bureau
Director Cinda Loucks
229-3271

General Services Bureau
Capt. Randy Oaks
229-3413

IT Operational Systems
Director Bambi Pilley
229-8383

Automation Policy and
Planning
Director David Garcia
229-3217

Human Resources Division
Deputy Chief Lou Pascoe
229-3234

Personnel Bureau
Exec. Director Doug Spring
229-3969

Training Bureau
Capt. Gary Schofield
229-3053

Professional Standards Division
Deputy Chief Mike Ault
229-3425

Quality Assurance Bureau
Capt. Marc Joseph
229-8373

Office of Employment
Diversity
Director Samantha Bethel
229-4147

Detention Services Division
Chief Paul Martin
671-3951

Records Bureau
Director Pat Schmitt
671-3913

South Tower Bureau
Capt. Marilyn Rogan
671-3958

Central Booking Bureau
Capt. Henry Hoogland
671-3960

North Tower Bureau
Capt. Mikel Holt
455-5141

Admin. Ops. Bureau
Steve Morris
671-3964

Law Enforcement Operations
Assist. Sheriff Mike Zagorski
229-3498

Central Patrol Division
Deputy Chief Carl Fruge
229-5699

Downtown Area Command
Capt. Ted Moody
229-4348

Southeast Area Command
Capt. Bob Chinn
229-3206

S. Central Area Command
Capt. Jim Dillon
229-8272

Airport Bureau
Capt. Mark Tavarez
229-3328

Trans. Safety Bureau
Capt. Rick Bilyeu
229-4073

Valley Patrol Division
Deputy Chief Cliff Davis
229-5755

Southwest Area Command
Capt. Tom Conlin
229-2843

Northwest Area Command
Capt. Gregory McCurdy
229-3426

Northeast Area Command
Capt. Stavros Anthony
229-3403

Bolden Area Command
Lt. Vincent Cannito
229-3347

Investigative Services Division
Deputy Chief Richard McKee
229-3511

Robbery/Homicide Bureau
Capt. Tom Lozich
229-3528

Crimes Against Youth/
Family Bureau
Capt. Terry Lesney
229-8376

Financial/Prop.
Crimes Bureau
Capt. Terry Mayo
229-5599

Criminalistics Bureau
Capt. Tom Hawkis
229-3471

Special Operations Division
Deputy Chief Bill Conger
229-3370

Homeland Security Bureau
Capt. Mike McClary
229-3253

Support Services Bureau
Capt. Marc Maston
229-3544

Vice and Narcotics Bureau
Capt. Frank Sutton
229-3461

Organized-Crimes Bureau
Capt. Dan Barry
229-5504

Index

About the Author

Dennis N. Griffin retired in 1994 after a 20-year career in investigations and law enforcement in New York State. He and his wife Faith moved to Las Vegas shortly afterward. Dennis wrote his first novel, *The Morgue*, in 1996. He currently has six published mystery thrillers, including the first two books of a Las Vegas-based trilogy. The author is an active member of the Mystery Writers of America, Las Vegas Valley Writers Group, Henderson Writers Group, and the Police Writers Association. For more information please visit www.authorsden.com/dennisngriffin.

About Huntington Press

Huntington Press is a specialty publisher of Las Vegas- and gambling-related books and periodicals. Contact:

Huntington Press
3687 South Procyon Avenue
Las Vegas, Nevada 89103
702-252-0655
www.huntingtonpress.com